Collector's limited edition

2,000 numbered registered copies

This copy is number __1388__

Cowboy Poetry

Classic Rhymes by
S. Omar Barker
(1894–1985)

Compiled by
Jodie and Bob Phillips
Edited by Mason and Janice Coggin
and Jon Richins

Cowboy Poetry, Classic Rhymes by S. Omar Barker (1894–1985)
Copyright © 1998 Marjorie and Robert Phillips
Compiled by Jodie and Bob Phillips
Edited by Mason and Janice Coggin and Jon Richins

Publisher:
Cowboy Miner Productions
P.O. Box 9674
Phoenix, AZ 85068
Phone: (602) 944-3763

Publisher's Cataloging-in-Publication Data

Barker, S. Omar 1894–1985.
Cowboy Poetry : Classic rhymes by S. Omar Barker / S. Omar Barker. Compiled by Jodie and Bob Phillips. Edited by Mason and Janice Coggin and Jon Richins
    p. cm.

ISBN: 0-9662091-9-2

1. Cowboy—Poetry. 2. Ranch life—Poetry. 3. West (U.S.)—Poetry
I. Title
Library of Congress Catalog Card Number: 98-88574

    02 01 00 99 98 5 4 3 2 1

Book Design & Typesetting: SageBrush Publications, Tempe, Arizona
Jacket Design: ATG Productions, Christy A. Moeller, Phoenix, Arizona
Printing: Bang Printing, Brainerd, Minnesota
Printed and bound in the United States of America

Acknowledgments

To our co-editor, Jon Richins, a big thank you for introducing us to S. Omar Barker's nephew, Bob Phillips, and his wife, Jodie. As co-editor, Jon has found gems written by Omar in old issues of magazines and newspapers. Thanks to Jon also for writing the articles on the inside flaps of the dust jacket.

To the Phillips family for gathering and preserving poems and stories written by Omar. We are also indebted to Jodie Phillips for contacting Elmer Kelton and asking him to write the foreword about his friend, Omar. Jodie spent long hours proof-reading the poems, another job greatly appreciated.

The logo for the Arizona Cowboy Poets Gathering inspired the cover illustration. Thanks to Warren Miller and his organization at the Sharlot Hall Museum.

Our thanks also go to Red Steagall, Duke Davis, Waddie Mitchell and Bob Christensen for their endorsements, and to many of our friends at the Cowboy Poets Gatherings across the United States who have encouraged us to put together this book on S. Omar Barker's poetry.

Contents

Tall Men Riding 15
The Tie-Fast Men 16
Cowboy Ridin' 17
Pants Polisher. 18
Big Windies. 20
Sometimes Serious 23
Cowboy's Complaint 24
Ol' Snoozy Schmidt 25
Code of the Cow Country 26
A Measure for Man. 27
Cowboy Breed 28
Grand Canyon Cowboy 30
Manana 30
Trail Dust. 31
Grass 32
Useless Question 33
Texas Truth 33
Horse Corral Etiquette 33
Hunted Men 34
Outlaw's Funeral 36
Spurs 37
Into the West. 38
Cry, Coyote! 39
His Night-Herd Pardner 40
Rangeland Sleepin' 41
Old Wagon Tracks 42
Against the Dark 43
Fine! 45
Judge Bean's Jury 46
Hangin' 47
Gun Law 48
Grave Error 49
Judge Bean's Bear. 50
Jurisdiction 52
A Letter From Judge Bean 53
Cowboy's Reverie. 57
Granger's Daughter. 58
Thirsty Cowboy. 60
To a Mountain Cowgirl 61
Mariposa Mesa 62

Bruin Wooin' 63
A Gal to Spark 66
The Sentimental Banker 68
Jack Potter's Courtin'. 70
Rangeland Perfume. 73
The Deputy's Star 74
One Way of Proposin' 76
Stew-Pified 77
To a Blue-Eyed Cowgirl 78
The Empty Bunk 79
Weddin' in Texas. 81
Vaquero's Valentine 85
Bedtime Story 87
Wearin' Daddy's Hat 88
The Ring-Tailed Wowser 89
Three Wise Men 91
Boy into Man 94
Ranch Mother 96
Watchin' Em Ride 97
Ranchman's Widow. 100
Curly Wolf College 101
Mountain Ranch Wife 102
A Frontier Wife 103
Ranch House Night 104
The Cowgirl at College 105
His First Shave 106
Cowpuncher Praise 107
Ravens Over the Pass 108
Bunkhouse Thanksgiving 111
Drifter's Thanksgivin' 113
Thanksgiving Argument 116
Draggin' in the Tree 118
Line-Camp Christmas Letter 120
A Cowboy's Christmas Prayer 122
The Cowboy's Religion 124
Drylander's Christmas. 125
Cowboy's New Year's Resolutions 126
Cow Country 129
The Chuckwagon 130
Black Magic 132
Buckaroo's Coffee 133
Hot Ir'n! 134
Quittin' Talk 136

Bear Ropin' Buckaroo	138
Fireside Windies	140
Boar's Nest Batcher	141
Canned Termaters	143
Power in the Pot	145
Bunkhouse Forum	146
Tenderfoot	148
What the Ol' Texan Misses	150
Old West Welcome	151
Hospital Cowboy	152
Texas Zephyr	154
Cowpuncher Caution	154
"Purt Near!"	155
Rodeo Days	159
The Winner	160
Agreement in Principle	160
Buckaroo's Squelch	161
Four-Footed Dynamite	162
What's a Bronco?	164
Mustang Manners	165
The Riders	166
Portrait of a Puncher	170
One or the Other	171
A Cowpuncher Watches the Crowd	172
The Bronc Buster's Epitaph	173
Horses Versus Hosses	175
Jughead	177
The Unpardonable Sin	179
Buckaroo Braggin'	180
Some Horses I Have Rode	181
Watchin' Him Drink	182
Namin' The Broncos	184
The Sparkin' Plug	185
The White Mustang	186
Longhorn	188
The Female of the Species	191
Cowpen Moo-Sic	192
The Last Bronc	195
Adios!	196
Old Cowboy	198
To an Old Cowboy—Departed (Jim Whitmore)	199
An Old Cowhand Enters Heaven	200
The Last Lone Trail	202

Foreword

How can anyone begin to tell who S. Omar Barker was?

The easy way would be to give the statistics: that he was born in a log cabin on a small mountain ranch at Beulah, New Mexico, in 1894, youngest of the eleven children of Squire Leander and Priscilla Jane Barker, that he grew up on the family homestead, attended high school and college in Las Vegas, New Mexico, was in his youth a teacher of Spanish, a high school principal, a forest ranger, a sergeant of the 502d Engineers in France in World War I, a trombone player in Doc Patterson's Cowboy Band, a state legislator and a newspaper correspondent.

That he began writing and selling stories articles and poems as early as 1914 and became a full-time writer at the end of his legislative term in 1925. That he married Elsa McCormick of Hagerman, New Mexico, in 1927, and she also became a noted writer of Western stories.

That he once estimated his career output at about 1,500 short stories and novelettes, about 1,200 factual articles, about 2,000 poems. That they appeared in a broad range of publications from the pulp magazines to such prestigious slicks as *Saturday Evening Post* and a varied array of general newspapers and magazines. That he did five volumes of poetry, one book of short stories and one novel, *Little World Apart* as well as one western cookbook with Carol Truax.

That the work probably best known to the general public was his poem, *A Cowboy's Christmas Prayer*, which has been printed more than one hundred times, recorded by Tennessee Ernie Ford and Jimmy Dean, and plagiarized more than once. That he won the Western Writers of America Spur award twice and was the 1967 recipient of the Levi Strauss Saddleman Award for bringing honor and dignity to the Western legend.

That in 1975 he was named an honorary president of WWA, of which he was one of the founding fathers and an early president. Elsa also served a term as president. That in 1978 he was the first living author to be inducted into the Hall of Fame of Great Western Writers in the National Cowboy Hall of Fame, Oklahoma City.

That he was known as the Sage of Sapello and the Poet Lariat of New Mexico.

That would be the easy way to tell about Omar Barker, but somehow it misses what we all felt about him, something beyond places and dates and titles published. It misses what he was as a person. He was many things to many people, but above all else he was a gentle man and a gentleman, a friend to everyone who knew him.

The only way I know to write about him is to tell what he meant to me.

I knew Omar's name from the time I was a boy growing up on a ranch in West Texas in the 1930s. My mother used to buy *Ranch Romances*, a bi-weekly Western pulp magazine. As soon as I caught her not looking, I would check to see if it contained a story about the boy Mody Hunter. For years, Omar did a humorous series about this lad who always seemed to be getting into trouble himself or getting other people out of it. Maybe I saw myself as Mody Hunter, or maybe as S. Omar Barker, because about that time I began to want to write stories myself. How much of that ambition to attribute to Omar I don't really know, but he was an influence.

Over the years that followed, his name was always among those I sought out when I picked magazines to read. I sensed that he knew what he was writing about because he wrote as my dad and all the cowboys around him talked.

Years later, the first fiction story I ever sold was to the very publication that I had read so much as a boy: *Ranch Romances*. It happened to be one of Omar's favorite magazines. He and Elsa wrote stories for years for its editor, Fanny Ellsworth.

After two or three of my stories were published, I received a note of congratulations from Omar and encouragement to do more. The thrill defies description. Other notes and letters followed. They could not have come at a better time, for more of my stories were still being rejected than bought. It would have been easy to chuck it all and resolve to make an honest living. There is no way to describe the lift a beginner gets from a pat on the back by a lifelong idol. I know now that Omar sensed this, and that I was by no means the only beneficiary of his generous spirit.

One night in the early 1950s I received a phone call from Omar. He and Elsa were spending the night in my town, San Angelo, on their way home from a trip. He asked if we would mind if they dropped by our house to get acquainted. Mind? I would have walked barefoot halfway to Las Vegas just to get to meet him.

They stayed a long time that night; we could not let them go. Omar gave me tips about writing that I have never forgotten and have used now for almost fifty years.

When WWA was organized, Omar was there, and he began very early to encourage me to join. I doubted that I had earned the credentials, but he and Tucson's Nelson Nye the self-styled "Baron of Blood and Thunder"—both leveled their sights on me and eventually persuaded me to join. I have been grateful to them ever since.

My debt to Omar is greater than I could ever repay. His work helped shape my vision when I was a boy. His kindness helped keep me going when I badly needed encouragement. And his insistence brought me into an association with other Western writers, one of the treasures of my life, personally and professionally.

His kindness did not stop there. Over the years he kept writing letters of congratulations or encouragement. At the WWA conventions he and Elsa always seemed to find a special time for Ann and me. And it was not just us. They made time for other young and struggling writers as well. It was not something they had to do or that gave them any personal reward, except probably a sense of satisfaction. They did it because of the kind of people they were.

And what a joy Omar was on the program at a convention! He was a master storyteller, his New Mexico mountain accent giving a perfect flavor to yarns we loved to hear over and over again, like the one about the tourist driving a little too fast down a winding road and coming all of a sudden upon a herd of cattle. Unable to stop, he desperately swerved first to the left, then to the right, managing somehow to miss everything except an old cow which stood broadside in the road. He knocked her rolling, and she landed in the ditch with all four legs in the air. As the tourist shakily got out of his car, a cowboy rode up. The tourist said, "I hope I didn't hurt her." Solemnly the cowboy replied, "Well, if you done her any good, I'll be glad to pay you for it."

Because he was bilingual—he had to be to serve in the New Mexico legislature in the 1920s—he had a stock of wonderfully innocent Hispanic stories, which he told in a delightfully soft dialect. It was a matter of regret to him in his later years that the telling of these grand stories, most learned from Hispanics of his own age, began to be frowned upon as politically incorrect, and he quietly retired them.

It is a matter of regret to me that younger writers have not had the great pleasure and privilege of getting to know Omar and Elsa, for his declining health—and later hers—prevented them from attending WWA meetings in their last years. Some of the finest hours I can remember at the conventions were spent with a small group of friends in a hotel room, where we would coax Omar into telling some of the gently risqué stories he was hesitant to relate to a large audience.

It is a pity more of his work is not readily available to readers today. Because so much of it was short, printed in magazines and newspapers and never reprinted in book form, it is lost to all but those who have the time and resources to dig it out.

He always used to joke that he intended to publish one more full-length book, a factual account to be known as *The*

Sons of Bitches of San Miguel County. The trouble was, every time he thought he had it finished, another one came to mind.

He made capital use of his own initials, which of course were S.O.B. The S stood for Squire, which he inherited from his father, but used only in the abbreviated form.

He edited several collections of stories on behalf of WWA and was generous in contributing his own work. An Omar Barker story or poem always added a little grace and humanity to any publication in which it appeared.

The last time Ann and I saw him and Elsa was on our way home from AWWA convention in Santa Fe. Even though Las Vegas was not far, his arthritis had become too painful for him to travel. He autographed a book for which he had written the introduction and added his brand, the Lazy SOB.

We received several letters from him in the months that followed. The handwriting was becoming shaky, and between the lines we realized he was saying good-bye. He died April 2, 1985. Elsa survived him by several years.

We have not really lost him. So long as friends remember him, and so long as fans can enjoy his work in collections such as this one, he will live.

No one who knew Omar Barker will ever forget him.

Elmer Kelton
San Angelo, Texas

(Mr. Kelton, a well-known Western writer has garnered many awards, the Golden Spur, the Saddleman and the Western Heritage Awards among those.)

Range Riders

Classic Rhymes by S. Omar Barker

Tall Men Riding

This is the song that the night birds sing
As the phantom herds trail by,
Horn by horn where the long plains fling
Flat miles to the Texas sky:

Oh, the high hawk knows where the rabbit goes,
And the buzzard marks the kill,
But few there be with eyes to see
The Tall Men riding still.

They hark in vain on the speeding train
For an echo of hoofbeat thunder,
And the yellow wheat is a winding sheet
For cattle trails plowed under.

Hoofdust flies at the low moon's rise,
And the bullbat's lonesome whir
Is an echoed note from a longhorn throat
Of a steer, in the days that were.

Inch by inch time draws the cinch,
Till the saddle will creak no more,
And they who were lords of the cattle hordes
Have tallied their final score.

This is the song that the night birds wail
Where the Texas plains lie wide,
Watching the dust of a ghostly trail,
Where the phantom Tall Men ride!

The Tie-Fast Men

This is the way of the tie-fast men,
    Where the unpenned cattle graze,
Where the coyote cries and mesas rise
    Through the blue of a far-off haze:
That whether the day be bright or gray,
    Blizzard or wind or sun,
Or the night pitch-black, they turn not back
    From riddle or ride begun.

In the canyon weeds the blue quail feeds
    Or whirs to the rocky hill,
And the pronghorn doe runs fast or slow
    To the whim of her wayward will;
But the men who ride where the range is wide
    Bend little to wayward whims.
In dust and sweat their code is set,
    Hard as the Caprock's rims.

When the rope is cast, the loop caught fast
    To honor or steer or friend,
The tie-fast crew are the cowboys who
    Stay tied to the other end.
And this is the rule of their rawhide school,
    Born of the roundup's dust:
"Once in your noose, don't turn it loose
    Till the doggoned cinches bust!"

This is the creed of a vanishing breed,
    To saddle and freedom born,
Their stout hearts tied to a rugged pride,
    Their ropes to the saddlehorn!

Cowboy Ridin'

I've rode where it's wet, I've rode where it's dry,
  I've rode the low country and also the high.
  I've rode for big outfits as well as for small,
  I've rode horses short, and I've rode horses tall,
  But ridin' that's *ridin'*, ol' cowpunchers claim,
  On ranch and on range is a heap more 'n a game.

I've rode some by night, and I've rode some by day,
  I've rode till my bottom felt plumb wore away;
  I've rode for good wages and also for pore,
  But no matter which, I know one thing for shore:
  They don't call it ridin, where western trails run,
  Unless there's some cow-work that needs to be done!

I've rode with a headache, I've rode with the itch,
  Got throwed off a few broncs that knowed how to pitch.
  I've warmed a few saddles with frost on my pants,
  And rode through a blizzard to git to a dance,
  But cowboys had just as well ride in a hack
  As ride with no ketch rope attached to their kack,
  To use, if they need to, on cow, calf, or steer,
  For ridin' ain't ridin' without ridin' gear!

I've rode where it's calm, and I've rode where it blows,
  I've rode in parades at rodeo shows,
  But ridin' ain't *ridin'*, ol' cowpunchers claim,
  Without cows to punch—and I figger the same:
  From Bighorn, Montana to old Albukirk,
  When cowfolks say "ridin," they're speakin' of WORK!

Pants Polisher

They asked me "What's a saddle?"
    So I told 'em it's a kack,
A rig of wood and leather
    shaped to fit a horse's back.
You set up in its middle
    with a leg hung down each side,
Some horse meat in between 'em,
    and that is known as "ride."

I could have stopped right there, of course,
    and saved a heap of steam,
But when they speak of saddles,
    my old eyes take on a gleam,
For the saddle is an implement
    that's bred a breed of man
Who rides the range of history
    plumb back to Genghis Khan.
Two legs was all us humans had,
    but men that wanted more,
They figgered out the saddle,
    and its magic gave 'em four.

The Saracen, the Cossack,
    the Arab and the knight,
The Mongol and the chevalier—
    they all was men of might,
Because instead of walkin'
    like a tamer breed would do,
They climbed up in a saddle
    when they had a job in view.

King Richard was a saddle man,
   and Sheridan and Lee,
And Grant and "Black Jack" Pershing—
   just to mention two or three.
Remember ol' Sir Galahad
   of that there poet's tale?
His pants was saddle-polished
   while he sought the Holy Grail!
Of course them heroes never rode
   no Texas applehorn,
But they're the cowboy's kinfolks,
   just as sure as you are born.

They asked me "What's a saddle?"
   It's a riggin' made to fit
A man (sometimes a woman)
   in the region where they sit.
It's made of wood and leather,
   with a cinch that goes around
A chunk of livin' horse meat
   'twixt the rider and the ground.
It's just the apparatus
   that a cowhand climbs upon
To start his day of cow work
   at the chilly hour of dawn.
It's just a piece of ridin' gear
   that, when it's had a chance,
Has give the world some heroes-
   while it polished up their pants!

Big Windies

They asked me "What's a windy?" . . .
    Well, us cowpokes love to spin
Our yarns around the campfire.
    Listen how them tales begin:
"Well, boys, I'm goin' to tell you
    'bout the time I hunted b'ar.
The fall work all was finished,
    so I took a *pasear*
Away up in the timber
    where the hoot owls have their fun,
To see if I could find some bear
    and maybe shoot me one.

The day was kinder warmish,
    so I laid down for a nap.
I woke up late that evenin'
    when I heard a great big snap,
And there beside me stood a bear—
    I tell you, boys, it's true—
This bear had took my rifle
    and he'd snapped it right in two!
He throwed the pieces at me
    as I shinnied up a tree,
Then give a grunt, spit on his hands
    and clumb right after me.

By that time it was gittin' dark.
   I reached the topmost limb.
That bear kept right on comin',
   so I knowed 'twas me or him.
Well, boys, that tree was mighty tall—
   a lucky thing, no doubt—
For by the time he got it clumb,
   ol' bruin's tongue was out.
A lollin' through his slobbers,
   such a tongue you never see,
As purty, pink and limber
   as a rubber singletree.
That's what I grabbed aholt of,
   and I swang him round and round
Until I yanked him inside out,
   then flang him to the ground.

But here's the part that's funny:
   I had started down when, wup!
Here come that doggone bear again,
   a-climbin' right back up!
Looked like he'd somehow turned hisself
   all right side out once more.
All I could do was grab his tongue
   the way I had before,
And yank him inside out again.
   I heard him hit the earth,
Then started squirlin' down that tree
   for all that I was worth.
But I'd no sooner started down
   than by the gobs I'll swear,
Tongue out and climbin' fast again,
   here come that doggone bear!

Well, boys, we kept right on that way
    until the break of day:
Ten times I yanked him wrong side out,
    but still he wouldn't stay.
At least that's what I figgered,
    but as soon as it was light
I saw what I'd been doin', boys,
    throughout the dark of night.
There lay upon the ground below—
    my word please do not doubt—
Not one but ten dead grizzly bears,
    all turned plumb wrong side out!"

"Big windies," if you'd like to know,
    are tales us cowboys spin
To kinder kill the lonesomeness
    when night comes closin' in:
About the mighty Pecos Bill,
    with cyclones in his loop;
About the wring-tailed wowser
    and the barbwire-tailed kadoop.
In fact the so-called "windy"
    of the well known cow range stamp,
Ain't nothin' but us cowpokes
    huntin' grizzly bears—*in camp*!

Classic Rhymes by S. Omar Barker

Sometimes Serious

There ain't no other breed of man around the world and back
That jokes as free as cowboys do, but still it is a fack
That settin' round the wagon when the stars ain't far away,
They sometimes talk as serious as a preacher on the pray.

"There's one ol' crick we all must cross," observes ol' Baldy Tim.
"And no man ever knows just when his turn will come to him;
But if I had my choosin' of the place I'm doomed to die,
I'd pick the highest mountain top, right up against the sky.
I might not git to heaven—that's a thing no man can tell—
But the devil sure would have to climb to round me up for hell!"

"Now me, I'm different thataway," says Llano Jim with pride.
"I'd ruther die in Texas where the plains is flat and wide,
For if so be there's hosses in that land we speak about,
I'd like to wake up ridin' where a man can stretch 'em out!"
Butch claims he wants his boots off, and he'd like to die in bed
Amongst his weepin' kinfolks, with a piller 'neath his head.
He's rolled up in a tarp so long out where the cattle range,
He'd kinder like to die abed—if only for the change.

They all express their 'druthers, with good reasons for the same,
Till Brazos Bill's the only one that ain't put in his claim.
He sets there kinder studyin' and scratchin' at his ham.
"Well, boys, where-at I'm due to quit, I just don't give a damn!
I'd just as soon 'twould be afoot as on a buckin' hoss.
The when, where, how, and what for—it is all up to the Boss.
To freeze up in a norther or to git drowned in a draw—
I just ain't got no 'druthers when it comes my time to taw.
I don't care what the place is, but I wisht I had the chance
To know its true location just a leetle in advance.
It might be near, it might be far, it wouldn't matter where,
But if I sure 'nough knowed the *place, I'd keep away from there!*"

Cowboy's Complaint

I wouldn't be a cowboy for a skunk-boat full of gold!
It's swim with sweat in summer an' it's freeze in winter's cold.
It's roll out with the morning star an' lace your saddle on
An' swaller bitter coffee long before the gray of dawn.

At snoozin' time for city folks, you step acrost your kack
To get your innards jolted as your pony warps his back.
It's round 'em up an' swing a rope an' wrestle down a calf,
An' earn your daily wages—'bout a dollar an' a half!

It's herd dust down your gullet with the air too thick to chew,
An' plenty times the water's such you've got to chew it, too.
It's set-fast on your hunkers an' your legs so sprung an' bent'
That your pants would fit a wagon-bow without no argument.

You eat so much hawg-boozem that a grunt's your greetin' hail,
An' you dassent take a look for fear yo've growed a curly tail!
It's take the ramrod's powders when he wants to swim the crick,
An' lean against a bullet when the rustlers try a trick.

It's hunt a trail or slide the groove or ride a lonely line,
It's cut the herd an' herd the cut an' watch for Injun sign.
It's lay upon a Tucson bed amongst the centipedes
An' dream about the easy life them city fellers leads.

I wouldn't be a cowboy for a skunk-boat full of gold—
It's 'cut a rusty' while yo're young an' 'cut back' when you're old.
"I wouldn't be a cowboy"—Thus the snort of Soogan Sam,
An' then he kinder grins and says, "I wouldn't—but I *am*"!

Ol' Snoozy Schmidt

A sleepin' fool was Snoozy Schmidt,
    The snorin' cowboy wonder.
He'd spread his bedroll wherever it hit
    And snooze through storm and thunder.
He'd sleep astride of a Texas kack,
    With a herd strung out behind him,
Or doze while he follered a rustler's track,
    Yet sometimes, maybe, find him.

He'd spool his roll full of cockleburs,
    And never a durn he'd care
If his piller was stuffed with a wowser's spurs,
    Or a centipede combed his hair.
When blizzards blowed till the wolves dropped dead
    On the wild plains bare and high,
You'd find ol' Snooze in a "Tucson bed,"
    Enjoyin' his ol' shut-eye.

The homesteaders came and they strung barbed wire
    Where the longhorns' trails had run,
And the prairie grass went up by fire,
    And men went down by gun.
But Snoozy Schmidt still got his rest.
    No trouble could make him weep,
For all he asked of the good Old West
    Was room for a man to sleep.

He never was much of a hand to fight.
    "Got nothin' to lose," he said.
"The plow can't hinder a cowboy's right
    To snooze in a "Tucson bed."
No headstone marks his grave, they say,
    As he sleeps through storm and thunder,
For he took a nap on the plains one day,
    And a homesteader plowed him under!

Code of the Cow Country

It don't take sech a lot o' laws
    To keep the rangeland straight,
Nor books to write 'em in, because
    They's only six or eight.

The first one is the welcome sign
    Wrote deep in Western hearts:
My camp is yours an' yours is mine
    In all cow country parts.

Treat with respect all womankind,
    Same as yuh would your sister.
Take care o' neighbor's strays yuh finds
    An' don't call cowboys "mister."

Shet pasture gates when passin' through;
    An' takin' all in all,
Be jest as rough as pleases you,
    But never mean nor small.

Talk straight, shoot straight, an' never break
    Your word to man nor boss.
Plumb always kill a rattlesnake.
    Don't ride a sorebacked hoss.

It don't take law nor pedigree
    To live the best yuh can!
These few is all it takes to be
    A cowboy an'.... a man!

A Measure for Man

I hear folks measure up their friends
    And foes, both men and ladies;
For some they foretell happy ends,
    For many, Hades.

This man, they say, is truly bad!
    He cusses and plays poker.
That fellow there is lost—poor lad—
    He's such a smoker.

That woman paints her face, and thus
    Her character besmirches.
(They pin the label "hell" on us
    Who dodge the churches).

They classify the bad and good
    By catalogues of vices
And smother human brotherhood
    In moral crises.

They growl at jolly songs we sing—
    Who knows what right or wrong is?
The human heart's a greater thing
    Than any song is.

Now here's a measure, friends, for man,
    That's short and sweet and snappy:
That one is good who, when be can,
    Makes others happy.

Forget the old vice catalogue—
    One evil's like another—
Thank God for every man—or dog—
    Who loves his brother.

Cowboy Breed

You take a bunch of cowboys
    when the bunkhouse stove is red,
Their tongues will come unsnaffled
    an' their talk will likely spread
To purt' near ever' subject
    that's been augured o'er an' o'er
Since Adam et the apple
    an' got choked upon the core.
'Twas such a wintry evenin'
    that we all let down our beard
An' owned up to the things in life
    of which each one was skeered.

Ol' Gig confessed it spooked him
    some to hear the coyotes howl.
He even felt some shivers
    at the screechin' of an owl.
"I'm skeered of water," Utah says.
    "although I've swum the crick,
To view a boomin' river
    makes my innards sorter sick."
Ol' Rusty claimed he'd spent
    his life a-dreadin' rattlesnakes,
An' jest to see one coilin' up,
    it shore give him the shakes.
Says Peeler Pete: "I'll tell you, boys,
    what skeers me, If I must:
I never mount a bronc
    but what I dread the cinch will bust!"

Rupe Hanley's been a sheriff
    an' there's notches on his gun;
If anybody's yaller,
    why he shorely ain't the one;

But when it come his turn to talk,
    right soberly he said:
"There's jest one thing I'm skeered of, boys:
    The other feller's lead.
It's true I've been a lawman,
    an' it's true I'll serve again
If ever hell is poppin'
    an' the sheriff calls for men,
It's true I'll stand an' face 'em
    when their guns is smokin' hot,
But all my life, I tell you,
    I've been skeered of gettin' shot!"

An' so it went around the stove
    till ever' feller told
Jest what the fearsome item was
    to make his blood run cold.
Ol' Gig, who claimed that coyote howls
    plumb raised his hackle-hairs,
Had never kicked at beddin' out
    with coyotes ever'wheres.
Ol' Utah spooks at water,
    but I've seen him swim a herd;
Ol' Pete, he busts the worst of broncs
    an' never says a word
About his fear of busted cinch;
    nor Rusty don't complain
About the snakes a cowboy sees
    on mesa, hill an' plain.

Rupe Hartley, he's a gunman,
    though he's skeered of gittin' shot.
Seems like the cowboy does his stuff
    in spite of fears he's got.
That's why, I kinder like the breed,
    the more of them I know.
There may be fear inside 'em,
    but they never let it show!

Grand Canyon Cowboy

I'd heard of the Canyon (the old cowboy said)
 And figured I'd like to go see it.
So I rode till I sighted a rim out ahead,
 And reckoned that this place must be it.

I anchored my horse to a juniper limb
 And crawled to the edge for a peek.
One look was a plenty to make my head swim,
 And all of my innards feel weak.

If I'd known how durned deep it was going to be,
 I'd have managed, by some hook or crook,
To tie my ownself to the doggoned tree
 And let my horse go take the look!

Manana

Manana is a Spanish word
 We all would like to borrow.
It means: "Don't skeen no wolfs today
 Wheech you don't shot tomorrow;
An' eef you got some jobs to did,
 Of wheech you do not wanna,
Go 'head an' take *siesta* now!
 Tomorrow ees manana!"

Classic Rhymes by S. Omar Barker

Trail Dust

Each age has had its heroes—
 men whose blood ran strong and red,
And some are lusty still today,
 and some have long been dead;
But whether on the land or sea,
 in blizzards or in gales,
No braver lads have ever been
 than those who rode the trails—
The trails from Texas to the North,
 whose hoofmarks now are gone,
With wild stampedes to quell at night
 and floods to swim at dawn.

Not days but months, across lone plains
 they trailed the herds along,
These saddle-men whose danger dust
 uprose mid laugh and song.
Oh, some were drowned by crossing floods,
 and some the blizzards froze,
And what some faced who did not die,
 the god of courage knows.
The tracks of trailing herds today
 are but time-hidden scars,
And trail dust long has mingled
 with the timeless dust of stars!

Grass

The cattle drifted seeking it 'cross plains and desert sand,
　Or bawled in driven trail herds when the drouth
Had shrivelled every blade and made the range a barren land,
　With thirst and hunger parching every mouth.

Grass, or unlucky lack of it, ruled cattle, men and life;
　Bold, independent cowboys were its slave,
And though it often drove them into hatred, death and strife,
　Unquestioning allegiance still they gave.

Cut fences, raided sheep camps, and the wars of ranch and range,
　Grim sixguns battles when they came to pass,
The old West's feuds and fellowships—
　　both sometimes weird and strange
Were marked with brand of water-hole and grass.

Two score brave men by balls of lead
　　sent swift to meet their God,
In Lincoln County's cattle war alone,
Lie, like the Kid, in lonely graves beneath south-western sod—
Do grass roots still entwine each crumbling bone!

Not tragedy alone has been its' vast heroic spawn,
For grass has fathered daring and romance;
And made a West of horseback men,
　　lean knights of leather brawn,
Whose trails are paths for progress far advance.

Oh, blades of grass are little things by every windlet whirled,
　By cricket song and kiss of rain caressed,
Yet they have ruled, since early time, the frontiers of the world!
Hail, Grass! The silent monarch of the West!

Useless Question

No Texan ever asks you where you're from. In fact they say
　　He views such questions as but idle chatter,
Because if you're from Texas, you will tell him anyway,
　　And if you're not, it really doesn't matter.

Texas Truth

Most cowpokes will tell you that here is a truth
　　You might as well learn in the days of your youth:
To be a cowpuncher you'll never learn how
　　Unless you are purt near as smart as the cow!

Horse Corral Etiquette

There's two kinds of jaspers, most cowboys agree,
　　They would purty near like to see hung:
The first waves his horse-ketchin' rope too damn free—
　　And the other one ditto his tongue!

Hunted Men

A cowboy rode up on his bald-faced pony.
His jaw was hard set and his gaze plumb stony.
"Well, howdy!" I hailed him. "I'm campin' alone—
Come set by my fire and we'll gnaw us a bone!"
"I've gnawed one too many already," he said.
"The law's on my trail and I ain't far ahead."
"'Tain't none of my business," I said, "But my friend,
The law-dodgin' trail never comes to an end.
You'll maybe ride now till you leave 'em behind you,
But if the law wants you, some day it will find you.
And even if not, do you want to grow older
Always a-lookin' back over your shoulder?"

"You're wastin' your wind," he said, "preachin' at me!
The border ain't far and I aim to go free!"
"The coyote," I told him, "thinks freedom is his'n,
Because he ain't locked in the walls of a prison;
But what kind of freedom is there to be bought at
The price that you'll always be hunted and shot at?"
This cowboy, he set there upon his bald pony
As stiff as a stick of uncooked macaroni.
"I ain't never stole," he said. "Ain't never lied;
But I shot me a man, and they're after my hide.
If your coffee is hot, kindly pour me a cup.
I'll drink it and ride on before they ketch up."
I poured him his coffee, a black cup and strong.
He drank it and rode on—a cowboy gone wrong.

Classic Rhymes by S. Omar Barker

I'm just an ol' trapper that camps out alone.
Ain't got any folks, and my name ain't my own.
I don't claim to judge what is wrong and what's right,
But when the high sheriff come ridin' that night,
I told him the likeliest kind of a tale
To throw him plumb off of that young puncher's trail.
I reckon it wasn't the right thing to do—
But how could I help it? *I've been hunted, too!*

Outlaw's Funeral

They didn't have no preacher
    When they laid Black Jack away,
For there wasn't much a preacher
    Could have figgered out to say.
Black Jack had been an outlaw,
    Till a bullet cut him down,
A scourge upon the highways,
    A terror to the town.

The gang that he had run with
    Wasn't there to see the sight
Of Black Jack being put to bed
    To sleep his last long night.
Six honest cowboys bore his pall,
    A plain, rough box of pine.
The most of them had smelt his smoke
    And heard his bullets whine.
No tears was shed, I recollect,
    And surely none was due.
Black Jack had been a bad'un,
    And his evil days was through.

Yet when the dirt was throwed
    Upon the grave wherein he lay,
One grizzly-headed cowhand
    Stepped forward with a spray
Old plain wild prairie flowers,
    And it didn't take him long,
For all he said was:
    "This is for a cowboy that went wrong."

Classic Rhymes by S. Omar Barker

Black Jack had been an outlaw,
    And the price he paid was fair,
But still 'twas mighty solemn
    Just to view them flowers there,
For we knowed that this ol' cowboy
    Had once been Black Jack's friend—
And he also was the sheriff
    That had brung him to his end.

Spurs

Jingling at well booted feet,
    Down the years they come,
Braver music than the beat
    Of a warlike drum.

Knightly swagger, gay romance
    In their tinkling song,
At the heels of mounted men,
    Booted men and strong.

Richard of the Lion Heart,
    Cavaliers Of Spain,
Wore this badge of chivalry—
    Clinking wheel and chain.

Lance and sword are crumbled rust,
    Armor glints no more,
Still the song of spurs is heard
    As in days of yore.

Jingling at the heels of men,
    Men of proud degree—
Cowboys, last of cavaliers,
    Booted men and free!

Into the West

I.
Traced in the flicker of greasewood fire,
The Cowboy Kid saw his heart's desire.
Still but a lad at a play cow camp,
His ears heard the milling remuda's stamp,
And he knew his heart would know no rest
Till he could scratch 'em along with the best;
And over the shouldered mesas ride,
His saddle a-creak with his horse's stride:
A boy a-dream for the time when he
Could answer the range's witchery.

II.
Huddled there by a hearthfire's flame,
Grizzled and old as a Salem dame,
His hair as whitish as alkali,
The Cowboy Kid sees his past go by.
He smells the sage from the mesa's rim,
And the days come tumbling back to him;
Days that were tanged with the smell of hair,
Burnt till the brand came clean and fair;
Nights that were droned with a milling herd—
His feeble heart within him stirred—
Out of the phantoms in the flame
Into his soul the old call came.

III.
Oh, a heart knows not when a body is old,
And riding days are a tale that is told—
For now he would saddle and over the hill,
Ride to the ranges that beckoned him still.
There by the fire as he fell asleep,
The old man's pulses ceased their sweep
Of cowboy blood through his leathered veins.
A West wind called from his sagebrush plains,
And off to dim ranges of mounted men,
The Cowboy Kid rode forth again.

Cry, Coyote!

Cry, coyote! Cry lonely at dawn
For days of a past unforgotten but gone;
For buffalo black on the wide, grassy plains,
In a land still unfettered by civilized chains.

Cry shrill for a moonrise undimmed by the glare
Of cities and highways. Who is there to share
With a slim little wolf all the longing he wails
From moon-mystic hilltops and shadowy trails?

Cry, coyote, gray ghost of the rimrock! Your cry
Still echoes in hearts where old memories lie.
Cry, coyote! Cry lonely at dawn
For open-range freedom now vanished and gone!

His Night-Herd Pardner

Oh, there're pardners good fer daytime
    and there're pals that's meant fer nights,
And a few that's good enough
    tah never change,
But fer me along in Maytime
    there Is only one jest right,
When I'm ridin' lonesome night herd
    on the range.

When a puncher gits to singin'
    kinder mournful like and low,
And there ain't no other sound
    but breathin' cows,
And the stars goes slowly swingin'
    like they've done since long ago,
And there ain't nobody round
    to make yuh rouse.

When a feller gits to dreamin',
    kinder happy-like and still—
Maybe foolish dreams
    he'd never want to tell
And the moonlight comes a streamin'
    frum behind some grassy hill,
Fer to put its touch of magic
    in the spell,

Then (o' course it's kinder lonely),
    but fer me a way out West,
While I'm ridin' herd
    in May or maybe June,
There's one silent pardner only
    that I'd pick frum all the rest:
My old pal and friend—
    the night-herd ridin' moon!

Rangeland Sleepin'

While pillows is softer fer under yer head
    Than bunch grass or ol' saddle leather,
An' maybe fer sleepin' a house an' a bed
    Is quite some pertection frum weather,

Still I kinder like it out here 'neath the stars,
    With slicker an' tarp fer pertection
With crickets a-twinkin' their cricket guitars,
    An' cattle in every direction.

My head on a saddle ain't pillowed so fine
    As yores may be there in the city,
But nobody's slumber is sounder than mine,
    An' I ain't no subject fer pity.

Because hard day ridin', hard pillows at night,
    Are earmarks, I reckon, of freedom.
Yer beds an' soft pillows are things of delight,
    But *cowpuncher* slumber don't need 'em!

Old Wagon Tracks

Those rain-washed gullies hid in grass,
    With ridges lined between—
Who sees them as our motors pass,
    Or reckons what they mean?
Smooth modern highways blot them out,
    Now that the far is near,
But they were once brave wagon trails
    Across a vast frontier.

See! There the old way winds the hill
    Our route now speeds around.
Death met them at its crest, and still
    The wagons held their ground,
And pressed ahead to mark the way
    For many a pioneer—
Dim trails that led America
    Across a last frontier.

Dodge City down to Santa Fe,
    The death road up the Snake,
The southern trail to Monterey—
    What price the route you take?
Our passage west is cheap today—
    Our fathers found it dear.
Old wagon tracks are battle scars
    Upon a lost frontier.

Against the Dark

Men make them fires against the night,
    For the dark must be withstood;
And the orange flame, the red, the white—
    Their wizardry is good.

The yellow blaze, the blue, the red,
    Beyond the builded wall.
And the black forest overhead,
    Against the starry sprawl—

Ever the darkened curtain lifts
    Where men squat close beside
A campfire, and the warm smoke drifts
    Along a mountainside.

The men who make them fires of wood
    Beyond the builded street,
May glimpse forgotten hardihood
    Where dark and fireglow meet.

And this is a magic thing to ken
    A god-thing, if you will:
That smothered flame may rise again
    From red coals glowing still!

Judge Roy Bean

Classic Rhymes by S. Omar Barker

Fine!

Judge Bean's court, knowed near and far,
  Was post office, billiard hall, and bar.
  Law and justice, whiskey and wine—
  All was noted upon his sign,
  And all was dealt with a high old hand
  Over this west-of-the-Pecos land.
  But Bean, as he swallered his ol' red-eye,
  Allowed that expenses was doggoned high,
  And so, for impudence, killin', theft,
  He laid on fines both right and left.

  Once ol' Bart, his right-hand man,
  Gallops in as hard as he can,
  Bringin' the news of a man shot dead
  Down by the Pecos' sandy bed.
  "By gobs, Bart, though it's kinder fur,
  I reckon I'll go as the coroner!"
  Sixteen miles the judge goes lopin',
  Sets on the body and says: "Court's open!"
  Searches a pocket and finds a gun,
  And twenty bucks in another one.

  "By gobs, boys, this coroner's court
  Finds 'twas an accident cut him short.
  And now, as the court of law and order,
  West of the Pecos and down to the border.
  I fine this corpse, for totin' a gun,
  Twenty bucks! And the case is done!"

  Under the shade of his spreadin' sign,
  Doin' his duty and likin' it fine,
  Ol' Judge Bean, with all his snortin',
  Made his court plumb self-supportin'!

Judge Bean's Jury

If times was bad or times was good,
  Ol' Judge Roy Bean done what he could,
  Out west of the Pecos, far away,
  To make both law and liquor pay.
  And it added a heap to his ol' enjoyment
  For all good men to have employment.

So that's how come, when he tried Joe Todd
  For stealin' a barrel of forty-rod,
  And Joe, he called for a jury trial,
  Judge Bean's whiskers bloomed a smile.
  "Bart," he says, "step out, by gobs,
  And all men found without no jobs,
  Fetch 'em straight to this here place
  To set on the jury in this here case!"

Nineteen men ol' Bart rounds up,
  But Joe Todd's lawyer, he says: "Wup!
  By all the law I ever knew,
  A jury is *twelve* good men and true!
  Just stop, Judge Bean, for a hasty look!
  You'll find the law there in your book.
  A jury of nineteen? Quite absurd!"

Judge Bean, he don't say nary a word
  Till he finds in his lawbook, page two-ten,
  That a jury consists of just twelve men.
  "By gobs, boys, that ain't good law!"
  Snorts ol' Judge Bean as he takes a chaw.
  "And bein' as it ain't, here's how I'll deal it:
  Tear out the page and plumb repeal it!"

With the page tore out, Judge Bean proceeds
To try Joe Todd for his evil deeds.
Nineteen men get jury jobs,
As ol' Judge Bean remarks: "By gobs,
Though *twelve* men might work a wee bit quicker,
Nineteen buys just a heap more liquor!"

Hangin'

They had a code on the old frontier,
   And most oldtimers heeded it.
They never did hang a man, I hear,
   Unless they thought he needed it.

Gun Law

Ol' Judge Roy Bean, out west of the crick,
Could hear a case an' judge it quick,
For he knowed the law like a J.P. ort,
With a bar to tend while a-holdin' court.
When the lawbook law didn't fit right good,
Ol' Bean could think of one that would.

Now amongst them Texas laws was one
Forbiddin' a man to carry a gun
Except when travellin', day or night—
To tote one *then* was plumb all right.
So a case come up where a wild young rip
Was charged with wearin' a loaded hip.

"I'm guilty, Judge, you can plainly see,
But first let the boys have a drink on me.
An' yore ol' pet bear looks thirsty, too—
I'll buy him a gallon of ol' keg brew.
I know that totin' a pistol is rash,
But the Court's got likker, and I've got cash
That's burnin' a hole in my Sunday pants
I'll spend it now while I've got the chance.
An' when I'm done these other gents
Will buy a round—with my compliments!
So step up, boys, an' wet yore lip,
For I've got hardware on my hip!"

Says the Judge, "One thing I've never spurned
Is a customer's cash. This court's adjourned!
I shore cain't accept no guilty plea,
An' I hereby set this prizner free.
For the law don't claim, an' it never will,
That you're *carryin'* a gun when you're standing still!
An' what's furthermore, by my unravellin',
Whenever you walk you're damn shore *travellin'*
An' a man that travels, by moon or sun,

Classic Rhymes by S. Omar Barker

Has got full rights to carry a gun!
The law on this here case is clear—
Step right up, gents, for booze or beer!"

Ol' Judge Roy Bean, out west of the crick,
He knowed the law—an' he made it stick!

Grave Error

Boot Hill was the pay-off, them old-timers claim,
For men that pulled triggers without takin' aim!

Judge Bean's Bear

Old-time trains on the S. P. Line,
 Down where the sands of the Pecos shine,
 Sometimes stopped at Vinegarroon
 Where old Judge Bean had a quaint saloon
 To which the passengers made a rush
 To sample his famous "rub-o'-the-brush."
 There, like as not, they'd pause to stare
 A'while at a big fat cinnamon bear
 Chained to a post with the shade so scant
 That the Texas sun made him puff and pant.

"That b'ar," ol' Judge Roy Bean would, grin,
 "Can do more tricks than a harlequin,
 But he won't perform, the smart ol' skunk,
 Till he's had some beer to make him drunk.
 He talks like a human, cusses, too,
 On about four quarts of good brown brew.
 If any of you gents would like to try it,
 I've got the beer—if you want to buy it."

It never failed! Some traveling gent
 With a wholesome hanker for merriment,
 Across the Lone Star bar *kerrplunk*,
 Would pay for beer to get the bear drunk.
 Four bits a bottle was Judge Bean's price.
 The beer looked good, and it gurgled nice
 As down the ol' bear's hatch it ran.
 "He'll talk putty soon just like a man—
 Just one more bottle will do the trick,"
 Judge Bean would grin, "if he gits it quick!"

Classic Rhymes by S. Omar Barker

One more bottle . . . Alas! Too late!
The train would whistle! It wouldn't wait!
As travelers ran to resume their trip,
Judge Bean would pull at his whiskered lip:
"Bart, git that b'ar in outa the sun.
He's sold some beer. We've had some fun.
Give him some meat—he's earned a chunk.
Do you reckon he ever would git drunk?"

Jurisdiction

At Vinegarroon, in Judge Bean's court,
    There warn't no long haranguin'.
Trial was quick and sentence short:
    A whippin', a fine, or hangin'.

The bar of liquor and bar of law
    Both shared Bean's humble shack.
He served both drink and justice raw,
    And neither one was slack.

But once a lawyer from San Antony
    Roused up some fuss and friction,
Claimin' this court was faked and phony,
    Without no jurisdiction.

The Judge just grins acrost his casks
    And calls up ol' Bart Gobble,
And of him this here question asks,
    With nary a wink nor wobble:

"If I say Bart, hunt up a tree
    And hang this prisoner to it,
By gobs, what would your answer be?"
    Says Bart: "Hell, Judge, I'd do it!"

"And suppose that I'm a-mind to string
    His lawyer too, by gob?"
"Why, Judge," says Bart, "if anything,
    Two'd make a neater job!"

"There, Mister Lawyer!" snorts judge Bean.
    "Cut out your balky-mulin'!
That's *jurisdiction* like I mean!
    Set down! For that's my rulin'!"

Classic Rhymes by S. Omar Barker

A Letter From Judge Bean

Judge Bean, he sold hard likker,
    an' the justice that he dealt
Was harder than the bullets
    in his rawhide cartridge belt.
His rulin's, they was final
    an' no mercy could be wrung
From Judge Bean's court,
    when cow thieves got their sentence to be hung.
Bart Gobble done the dirty work,
    as to the thirsty crowd
The Judge dispensed hard Iikker.
    There was no appeals allowed,
From this an' other doin's
    an' the way he cussed at Bart,
Yuh might surmise that ol' Judge Bean
    was plumb without a heart.

But once a German mother
    wrote to ask about her son.
Her boy, she said, had run away,
    an' though plumb full of fun,
She knowed he wasn't bad at heart;
    an' somehow she had heard
That he'd been saw at Langtry,
    and she hoped to get some word.
The Judge, he combed his whiskers
    an' he stooped to start a bung,
An' he gazed out through the window
    to a propped up wagon tongue.
Frum which there swung an' outlaw
    with a good ol' German name
Who'd robbed an' stole an' murdered
    an' been strung up fer the same.

"Well, now by gobs!" the Judge remarks,
    "he got his legal dues
But his pore ol' grievin' mother
    won't rejoice none at the news."
But she'd wrote to Langtry's mayor,
    which was one of ol' Bean's jobs.
An' he kinder had to answer,
    so he says, "Well, now by gobs,
Go call me in a writer
    whilst I close this likker store,
Fer I'm goin' to write a letter
    'bout a boy that is no more!"
So the Judge he framed a letter,
    with the help of Billy Dodd,
An' he told the outlaw's mother
    how her son lay 'neath the sod—

An' how the sun of Texas
    shone down proudly on his grave,
An' all men done him honor
    as a hero, true an' brave.
He said he'd knowed him mighty well,
    a true friend, fair an' square,
An' ever in a fight fer right,
    her fearless son was there.
An' finally he told her
    how a bullet struck him down
While he stuck to his duty
    as the Marshal of the town.
An' how all stores in Langtry
    (Bean's saloon the only one)
Had closed their doors in mourning
    fer her noble, martyred son.

Then next day ol' Bean opened up,
    an' to the crowd he read
The letter him an' Bill had wrote.
    "An' now, by gobs," he said,
"Yuh may believe this letter
    an' you may believe it not,
But the first 'un to dispute it—
    this here court'll have him shot!"
They say Judge Bean was heartless,
    but a mother, old and gray,
Took comfort from his letter,
    wrote in Langtry, fur away.

Courtin'

Classic Rhymes by S. Omar Barker

Cowboy's Reverie

There's a lone night bird a-calling,
    There's a low moon o'er the hill,
Down the draw I hear cattle bawling,
    And a wind that is never still.

From afar lamplight is gleaming,
    Phantom light beyond a dim vale—
But it's all just lonesome dreaming
    On a lone cowboy trail.

There's a lone coyote a-calling
    To his mate out on the plain,
And the stardust on my heart falling
    Brings you back to my arms again.

Dreams of love long past redeeming
    Stir again at that wistful wail
Just a lone cowpuncher dreaming,
    On a lone cowboy trail . . .

Granger's Daughter

I spied a granger's daughter
    as the herd come up the trail.
Her pa looked raw and bony,
    and her ma looked g'ant and pale.
I seen her at the dugout door
    amidst a lonesome land,
And the herd dust sorter choked me
    when I seen her wave her hand.

I spied a granger's daughter
    standin' in a dugout door,
I seen her clothes was ragged,
    then I didn't see no more.
The hand she waved was little,
    and it sorter makes me sweat,
A-ridin' 'round the herd at night—
    seems like I see her yet.

I said her hand was all I seen.
    It's been a week by now.
Seems like I also seen her eyes,
    though damned if I know how.
I study on her, standin' there
    to watch the herd come through,
And wonder how the hell I know
    her eyes were soft and blue.

The herd dust rose between us
    like a fog upon the air,
But I mayhap glimpsed the glimmer
    of her yaller-golden hair.
I know about them grangers,
    how they ration mighty scant,
And it seems to me her features,
    they was sweet but sorter g'ant.

Classic Rhymes by S. Omar Barker

There's fancy gals in Abilene
    and buxom gals back south,
But me, I keep on thinkin'
    of the sweet and wishful mouth
Of a lonesome little granger
    as she watched me ridin' by,
From the doorway of a dugout
    on the plains of alkali.

I spied a granger's daughter
    as the herd come up the trail,
And it's lonesome on the prairie
    when you hear the coyotes wail.
There's fancy gals in Abilene,
    but when I draw my pay,
I'm headin' for a dugout
    that we passed upon the way!

Thirsty Cowboy

There's a sayin' out West, and it's true, I'll allow,
  That a man who can't drink from the track of a cow
Ain't much of a cowboy; for where punchers ride,
There ain't babblin' brooklets on every side,
For a waddy to drink from when joggin' around.
He waters, like cattle, wherever it's found.
Sometimes there is gyp in the water he drinks;
Sometimes it is muddy, and sometimes it stinks.
Sometimes it's so thick where the cattle have pawed
That before it is swallered it has to be chawed.

But speakin' of water and cowpuncher thirst,
I'll tell you when cowpokes get thirsty the worst.
It's when, at a slow walk that's known as *andante*,
He's passin' in sight of some homesteader's shanty,
And yonder beneath a blue sunbonnet shows
The face of a nester gal hangin' out clothes.
Or maybe he glimpses her framed in the door,
Her yaller hair gleamin' like gold-bearin' ore,
And all of a sudden her face looks so pink,
His terrible thirst makes him stop for a drink.

He may have just drunk from a spring cold and clear
A half a mile back—and the drink he'll get here
May be tanky-warm; but the dipper it's in
Is handed to him by a gal with a grin
That's sure mighty friendly—though modest and shy.
So he drinks and he drinks like he sure 'nough was dry.

Then maybe he lingers a minute or two
And talks about horses, the way cowboys do,
Until, by the time he gets ready to leave,
She's noticed a button that's loose on his sleeve.
So she sews it back on. Well, that's how it goes
When a cowboy sees a nester gal hangin' out clothes!
For nothin' else makes him so thirsty for water
As a glimpse of a homesteader's pretty young daughter!

To a Mountain Cowgirl

My cowgirl gal's a mountain maid,
    Perhaps that's why her eyes
Are deep as lakes in spruce-tree shade
    Beneath clear mountain skies.

Her range is up where Mother Earth
    Is mostly stood on edge,
An' trails cling like a saddle girth
    To every dizzy ledge.

Where cow trails through green aspen groves
    A-shimmer with hill rains,
Are bower paths for lady-loves,
    Soft shadowed lovers' lanes.

Oh, she's as slim as mountain fir,
    As true as mountain pine,
As shy as grouse in juniper,
    As sweet as columbine!

The plains look up at sunset hills
    And for far high trails sigh,
As if they longed for mountain thrills—
    Who blames them?—So do I!

Mariposa Mesa

There's a high green mesa where the mariposa blooms
    An' it ain't far up to the sky,
Where the wind's a purrin' pussy an' the wild grouse throoms,
    An' the bunch grass grows thigh-high.

There's plains off in the distant east, an' pilin' in the west,
    There's snow-eared peaks a-juttin' in the blue.
The boss's cows are sleek an' fat a-grazin' while I rest
    An' dream each mariposa bloom is you.

The boss, he comes a-ridin' by a-lookin' plumb content.
    Says somethin' 'bout "sech damn fine feed."
But me, though I'm a puncher an' I gathers what he meant,
    It's jest the pretty flowers that I heed;

Because, well—jest because—I,' guess—
    because—I'm plumb in love!
    Right pretty things jests sets me in a whirl,
An' mariposa blossoms with the blue, blue sky above,
    Reminds me of my cowgal girl!

An' so on high green mesas with their mariposas tall,
    (Though it is damn good range there, too!)
It ain't the grazin' qualities that holds me in their thrall!
    It's the bloomin' flow'rs that make me think of you!

Classic Rhymes by S. Omar Barker

Bruin Wooin'

The track of the bear that had killed Carson's pig,
It wasn't so small and it wasn't so big
But what when this cowboy come ridin' a-past,
He claimed he'd go git him—an' go git him fast.

"The dogs took his trail," the nester gal said.
"But Pa couldn't make it—he's down, sick abed.
We'd be mighty glad if you'd foller the dogs
And shoot that ol' bear 'fore he gits all our hogs!"

"Well, ma'am," says the cowboy, a gleam in his eye,
"To please a fair maid, there ain't much I won't try,
For I'm Bill Maginnis, a buckaroo which
Kills panthers bare handed and bears with a switch!
So if this pig-killer ain't handy to shoot,
I'll grab me a tail holt and pop off his snoot!"

And so, spizzered up by the nester gal's smile,
Bill rode up the canyon not more than a mile,
And there found the nester's dogs bellerin' brave,
A-bayin' that bear in a little ol' cave.
To git to this openin' up there in the rocks,
Bill had to shuck boots and climb in his socks.

The ledge was plumb narrow, the cave mouth was small.
Bill stooped to peek in and saw nothin' at all,
For to this here hunter of bears with a switch,
All inside the cavern was darker than pitch.
The nester's two mongrels kept raisin' a din
Around the cave's mouth, but they wouldn't go in.

Ol' Bill tried to "sic 'em," but them dogs was wise.
They wouldn't go in—and the look in their eyes
Was purt near reproachful, up there on the shelf,
As much as to say: "Whyn't you try it yourself?
We've holed up your bear—that's all we can do!
If you want him *un*holed, mister, that's up to you!"

Bill knowed by the smell he was in there all right.
He struck him a match and peered in by its light.
Two little red eyes in the glow was reflected—
And then somethin' happened Bill hadn't expected:
A sweet maiden's voice drifted up from the crick:
"Could you poke the bear out if I hand you a stick?"

The nester's fair daughter had follered to view
A bear gittin' switched by her bold buckaroo.
The sight of this maiden shore give Bill a sweat,
Recallin' some braggin' he'd like to forget.
But you take a cowboy, and what he won't try
To dazzle a damsel's admirin' blue eye!

"I'll crawl in an' git him!" Bill's voice was plumb bold
In spite of the blood in his veins runnin' cold.
"I'll grab a tail-holt and I'll show you the art
Of whip-snappin' bears till they plumb fly apart!"
But when he stooped down—with his hand on his gun
'Twas bruin hisownself that started the fun.

With a growl and a squall and a big whoosh of wind
He came out of there like a cat bein' skinned.
Bill riz up plumb sudden, his legs spraddled wide,
To find hisself straddlin' a hairy black hide.
The bear give a beller, Bill's gun give a boom,
They both give a lurch, and the dogs give 'em room.

Bill wrastled the bear and the bear wrastled him.
Bill grabbed for the tail-holt—and fell off the rim!
And who was on top as they rolled down the hill?
Sometimes it was bear and sometimes it was Bill!
Then just when pore Bill thought his last blood was shed,
The gal grabbed his pistol and shot the bear dead!

Bill lived to git married—a right happy hitch—
His wife, she won't let him hunt bears with a switch.
Now this story's moral, if moral you crave,
Points straight at you hombres that talk up too brave.
It's a plenty good rule, Mister Big-Braggin' Male:
When wrastlin' a bear, never reach for his tail!
Though reasons for this are both mighty and many,
It's mainly because he ain't got hardly any!

A Gal to Spark

I've picked me out a gal to spark,
    Like every feller ort—
Her chin looks kinder longish
    And her feet ain't none too short.
I called last Sunday evenin'
    And some other fellers come,
And all we done was talk of cows
    And watch her chaw her gum.
She kept her rocker squeakin'
    Till you'd think she'd wear it out,
And listened to us speakin'
    Of the grass and of the drought;
But when I told about the cow
    That claimed me for her calf,
It kinder warmed my gizzard
    Jest to hear her friendly laugh.

A yaller moon come boomin' up,
    We heard a kiote howl,
And from the ghosty hills
    There come the hootin' of an owl.
So there we set in silence,
    Thinkin' lonesome thoughts, I guess,
About the cowboy's lonesome life,
    So rough and comfortless.
Then purty soon we rolled some smokes
    Like cowboys always do,
And got our broncs and rode away,
    The whole dang bashful crew.
But me, I'm goin' back again
    'Most ever' chance I git,
And set there on the porch with her
    Till all them others quit.

I've picked me out a gal to spark,
    For lone trails lie ahead—
Her build is kinder buxom
    And her elbows kinder red.
There's pictures in the cattylogs
    Of gals with wavy hair,
While hers is straight and yaller—
    But I shore as hell don't care!
She rocks her rawhide rocker
    Till you'd think she'd wear it out,
But when I talk of cows
    She knows jest what it's all about.
Her face ain't got the beauty
    That it takes to win a prize,
But there's shore a heap of kindness
    In the way she bats her eyes.

I've picked me out a gal to spark—
    My love has done been found!
I shore do aim to win her—
    She's the only one around!

The Sentimental Banker

I went to see a banker
    to negotiate a loan.
He asked me how much land
    and cows and hosses did I own.
I told him all the land I owned
    was on my dirty neck,
And would he please get down to biz
    and write me out a check!
His cold eyes looked me over,
    and his face was like a rock.
"No land?" he says. "Well, then
    perhaps your brand is on some stock?"
"I've got one hoss and saddle, sir,
    one lass rope and the itch.
Ten thousand cows is all I need
    to make me fairly rich;
Two hundred head of hosses
    for my buckaroos to ride,
And maybe run a bank or two
    for money on the side;
A goat ranch down in Texas
    and some sheep in Idaho
Would help a feller through a pinch,
    but as you doubtless know,
A dogie is a calf that cannot choose
    which cow he sucks,
And neither can a cowboy
    when he's needin' fifty bucks!"

"A-hem . . . a-hum . . . the banker says.
    "You own no stock nor land
To offer as security!
    I hope you understand
The principles of finance
    and the law of quid pro quo,
By which we must be guided
    in the lending of our dough."

"Why, sure," I says.
   "I savvy that a loan is hard to git
Except when you are plenty flush
   and not a-needin' it.
But all I want is fifty bucks
   to jingle in my jeans
And make that gal I'm courtin'
   think that I can buy the beans
To feed us when we're married.
   So I'll tell you what I'll do:
As soon as we have got ten kids,
   I'll mortgage five to you!
Meantime I ain't got nothin'
   that will guarantee your bet,
Except the monthly wages
   of my own cowpuncher sweat."

This banker looked me over
   from my boot heels to my neck,
Then kinder grinned and took his pen
   and wrote me out a check.
"The principles of finance,"
   he remarked, "perhaps allow
A little leeway now and then.
   I've also punched some cow
When I was somewhat younger,
   but I never saved a cent
Until I got myself a wife
   to watch how it was spent!"

I went to see this banker—
   in a way, I must have blundered.
I only asked for fifty bucks—
   he passed *me out a hundred!*

Jack Potter's Courtin'

Now young Jack Potter was a man
    who knowed the ways of steers,
From bur-nests in their hairy tails
    to ticks that chawed their ears.
A Texican and cowhand,
    to the saddle bred and born,
He could count a trail herd on the move
    and never miss a horn.

But one day on a tally,
    back in eighteen-eighty-four,
He got to actin' dreamy,
    and he sure did miss the score.
The Trail Boss knowed the symptoms.
    "Jack, you ain't no good like this.
I'll give you just ten days
    to go and find out what's amiss!"

A "miss" was just what ailed him,
    for he'd fell in love for sure
With a gal named Cordie Eddy
    mighty purty, sweet and pure.
So now Jack rode a hundred miles,
    a-sweatin' with the thought
Of sweetsome words to ask her with,
    the way a feller ought.

"I'm just an humble cowhand,
    Miss Cordie, if you please,
That hereby asks your heart and hand,
    upon my bended knees!"
It sounded mighty simple
    thus rehearsed upon the trail,
But when he come to Cordie's house,
    his words all seemed to fail.

'Twas Howdy, ma'am, and how's the crops?
    And how's your pa and ma?"
For when it come to askin' her,
    he couldn't come to taw.
He took her to a dance one night.
    The hoss she rode was his.
"He's a dandy little horse," she says.
    "Well, yep," says Jack, "he is."

They rode home late together
    and the moon was ridin' high,
And Jack, he got to talkin'
    'bout the stars up in the sky,
And how they'd guide a trail herd
    like they do sea-goin' ships,
But words of love and marriage—
    they just wouldn't pass his lips!

So he spoke about the pony she was ridin',
    and he said:
"You'll note he's fancy-gaited
    and don't never fight his head."
"He's sure a little dandy!"
    she agrees, and heaves a sigh.
Jack says: "Why, you can have him—
    that is—maybe—when I die."

He figgered she might savvy
    what he meant or maybe guess,
And give him that sweet answer
    which he longed for, namely "yes."
But when they reached the ranch house,
    he was still a-wonderin' how
He would ever pop the question,
    and he had to do it now.

Or wait and sweat and suffer
    till the drive was done that fall,
When maybe she'd be married,
    and he'd lose her after all.
He put away her saddle,
    led his pony to the gate:
"I reckon I'll be driftin', ma'am.
    It's gittin' kinder late."

Her eyes was bright as starlight,
    and her lips looked sweet as flow'rs.
Says Jack: "Now this here pony—
    is he mine, or is he *ours?*"
"*Our* pony, Jack!" she answered,
    and her voice was soft as moss.
Then Jack, *he* claims he kissed her—
    but she claims he kissed the hoss!

Classic Rhymes by S. Omar Barker

Rangeland Perfume

There's something in the tang of things
    That makes a feller feel
For home or for adventurings,
    For woe or maybe weal.

Thus some will crave to smell the sod
    Turned over by a plow;
To them that fish the stink of cod
    Is pleasant, I'll allow.

I've whiffed the scent of city streets,
    Of dreamy-sweet perfumes
Where silk-lined ladies buys their eats
    In whisper-lighted rooms.

I know why sailors love the tang
    Of whippin' sprays at sea,
But still them smells don't bring no pang
    Into the heart of me.

But when the cows gits rollin' fat,
    And autumn's on the hills,
The rangeland spreads a perfume that
    Fair warms my soul with thrills.

Oh, sage brush in the yaller bloom
    Brings back the memory
Of evenings, where lone mesas loom,
    When she would ride with me.

And so I'm sendin' her a branch
    Down to that city school.
She is been a year gone from the ranch,
    And maybe I'm a fool,

But I'll bet all my yearlin' herd
    That when she smells that tang
We used to love, without a word
    She'll let the school go hang!

The Deputy's Star

When you've rode to town for sparkin',
    But the sheriff calls you in,
And he says he's had his eye on you,
    And never cracks a grin,
Why, it sorter riles your dander,
    And it loosens up your jaw,
Till you lay it off right salty
    What you think about the Law!
For you figger he's referrin'
    To some ruckus that you've had,
And he aims to jail you for it,
    And it makes you mighty mad.

But he lets you do your squawkin',
    Gazin' thoughtful at his feet,
Then he asks about that gal of yours
    A-waitin' up the street.
Do you sure 'nough aim to marry her?
    And is she just a fluff,
Or would she stick beside you
    If the goin' got right tough?
Well, you start once more to cuss him,
    But you don't get very far,
For his hand comes from his pocket
    With a new and shiny star.

Classic Rhymes by S. Omar Barker

He steps up sorter solemn,
    And he pins it on your vest,
And he says a man your caliber
    Can surely meet the test.
He's sorter took you by surprise.
    You don't know what to say,
So the ol' boy says it for you
    In his grim but kindly way—
He says the star means danger
    And a-ridin' trails that's hot,
With your woman home a-waitin'—
    If you get back safe or not.

For the Law will be your master,
    And he knows you'll serve it true. . . .
Up the street your gal's a-waitin' . . .
    What the hell's a man to do?
Well, the star's done pinned on solid,
    And you just can't yank it off!
Will she be as proud as you are?
    Will she weep? Or will she scoff?
So you're somehow mighty happy
    When she holds you extra tight,
And her lips are all a-quiver—
    But she says the star's all right!

One Way of Proposin'

Oh, Sue was young and Sue was fair
    and Sue was slim and neat.
She helped support her crippled Dad
    by servin' stuff to eat
To hungry cowboys stoppin' in,
    from wranglin' stock all weary,
And plenty of us hankered hard
    to have Sue for our dearie.

Most specially young Bashful Burt,
    a tophand with the herd,
But too ungodly modest
    to attempt a courtin' word.
She turned the rest of us plumb down,
    so sweet it hardly hurt,
And then we seen the way it was—
    she hankered after Burt!

And him all blush and bashfulness,
    the pore cowpunchin' sinner,
He had her won already
    but was still too dumb to win her.
Then one fine day a drummer guy
    breezed in for noonday chow,
And growled about the service
    like he hankered for a row.

The fare was beans—and mighty fine.
    I know, for I was there.
But this here uppish drummer bowed his neck
    and pawed the air.
Shoved back his beans plumb unpolite:
    "I ain't no hired help!
Bring me some food that's civilized!"
    You should of heard him yelp.

Classic Rhymes by S. Omar Barker

Pore Sue looked all beflustered.
    Then Burt riz up in his jeans,
Drawed out his gun and calmly says:
    "Now stranger, eat them beans!'
Then Sue looks up adorin'
    and toward Burt kinder leans,
Till all at once he kisses her—
    and the stranger eats his beans!

Stew-Pified

Potluck Pete, since he's been wed,
    Claims he's been so darned well fed
On good beef stew by his new bride
    That love has got him stew-pified!

To a Blue-Eyed Cowgirl

I used to think the sky was blue,
    And mornin' light was neat,
Before I saw the eyes of you
    Sun-smilin' clean and sweet.
But now .... gee whiskers .... I don't know—
    Somehow the things I see
In your blue eyes jest seem to glow
    With happiness fer me!

Seems like I see the spring sky there,
    An' twilight soft and gray.
An' cabin smoke curled in the air
    That quiet kind of way
It sometimes does from happy homes
    Back in the grassy hills.
To sech like things my fancy roams,
    My heart with wishin' fills.

Jest seein' things, there in your eyes,
    I never dreamed before.
A little ranch—not much fer size—
    You, waitin' at the door.
Or mebbe on my pinto hoss
    Some days you'd come an' ride—
I'd be the foreman, you the boss,
    Trail-driftin' side by side.

One-time "sky blue" meant sky to me.
    Now, it's the eyes of you
All full of happy things to be
    An' dreams we'll make come true.

Classic Rhymes by S. Omar Barker

The Empty Bunk

Ol' Charley's boots with saggin' heels
    stand empty by his bunk,
And yonder hangs his ol' guitar—
    we shore do miss its plunk.
We've done rolled up his soogans
    from the bunk he'll use no more.
We couldn't hardly sleep last night
    for missin' Charley's snore.
This bunkhouse on the ol' Bar G,
    it somehow ain't the same
With Charley's chuckle missin'
    from the ol' casino game.
His hawgleg shore looks lonesome
    in its holster on the wall,
For a gun without its wearer, why,
    it ain't no gun at all!
Bud claims ol' Charley got his dues—
    he rode too much at night.
There's danger in such doin's
    when the moon is shinin' bright.
But me and Spike, we both agree,
    whoever was to blame,
We shore will miss ol' Charley,
    and 'twill never be the same
As when he used to cuss the cook
    for callin' us at dawn,
Yet roll out with a grin on.
    Why, we cain't believe he's gone!

Ol' saggin' boots that's empty
    and an ol' hat on a nail,
While out acrost the valley
    you can hear the kiotes wail
As if they too was grievin'
    for the sound of Charley's song
That kinder cheered the bunkhouse
    when the winter nights was long.

So here we sadly set tonight
    and ponder on the days
When Charley, wild and woolly,
    with his pistols both ablaze,
Rode squawlin' into town with us
    a-shootin' in the air,
To show the world we're curly wolves
    with cactus in our hair.
But Charley's saddle's cold tonight,
    he'll gallyhoot no more,
For yonder hangs his pistol
    on a nail behind the door.
He's done forsook the Boar's Nest,
    with a grin upon his face,
And left his puncher plunder here—
    to clutter up the place.
It's kinder sad to view it,
    where he left it, dang his hide,
To travel off to Texas,
    honeymoonin' with his bride!

Weddin' in Texas

The wedding guests were gay that night
    with josh and joke and quip,
But every man among them
    wore a sixgun at his hip.
For this was Texas long ago,
    when blood ran hot and fast,
When men who lived by horse and gun
    loved frolic to the last.

The bride and groom led off the dance.
    It was a joy to see
The blithesome blushing of the bride
    of young Joe Sitterlee.
The caller with his rusty twang,
    the fiddler with his bow . . .
"Now rope that heifer, swing her high!
    Now swap and do-see-do!
Now sop your gravy, spoon your sass!
    Now pat her on the head!
Now turn that heifer out to grass
    and circle like I said!
Now hug your honey fit to kill
    and stomp acrost the floor!
Now—" Suddenly the room was still.
    A man stood in the door.

"Well, Ranger Hall," Bill Meador said,
   "what's itchin' in *your* pants?"
"I guess you know," the Ranger drawled,
   "I didn't come to dance.
I've come to take the seven men
   who killed ol' Doc Brazell.
I'll read the list of them I want."
   A curse—"You will, like hell!"
Joe Sitterlee it was who spoke.
   "You're on the list," said Hall.
"We've got the place surrounded, boys!
   We aim to take 'em all!"
"Not much, you won't!" Bill Meador snarled.
   "This is Joe's weddin' night!
You want to leave here 'live—or dead?
   We're fixed to make a fight!"

"You've named the dog," shrugged Ranger Hall.
   Then loud they heard him say:
"They're clearin' out the women, boys!
   Git set to blaze away."
"Our powder's dry!" his men called back
   from outside in the gloom.
Then, pale as death, the bride came forth
   across the thinning room.
"This is my wedding night," she said.
   "I'll n'er have one again.
Please let the wedding dance go on,
   then take your wanted men!
A court of law might free my Joe—
   that chance I'll choose to take,
For if he fights and dies tonight,
   my heart will surely break!"

Classic Rhymes by S. Omar Barker

The dance went on, and it was gay
    with josh and joke and quip,
But now no one but Rangers
    wore a sixgun at the hip.
The caller's rusty twang rang out
    above the fiddle's wail:
"You better swing them heifers now!
    There won't be none in jail!"
For this was Texas long ago,
    when blood flowed hot and fast,
When men who lived by horse and gun
    loved frolic to the last.

Families

Vaquero's Valentine

I rode a buckskin pony
    and she rode a nester's mule,
When both of us was scholars
    at the ol' Red Canyon school.
Her seat was right in front of mine.
    I never will forget
The valentine I brung her—
    paper lace like mignonette,
And crimson hearts and cupids—
    how her blue eyes opened wide
When she found the ring-tailed lizzards
    I had hid for her inside!

She used to bring me peanuts,
    But how she'd stomp my toes
Because some hulls got down her neck.
    she had a turned up nose,
And eyes about the purty blue
    of mountain columbine.
She slapped me some for callin' her
    my red-haired valentine.
I'd let her ride my pony,
    but there sure was heck to pay
When I burred the saddle blanket
    and he bucked her off one day.

She drawed a comic valentine
    of Teacher wearin' pants;
The Teacher took it from the box
    And kinder looked askance.
The one that drawed such nonsense,
    was the Teacher's stern decree,
Would have to take a whippin'—
    so I up and said 'twas me.
I'd of took the whippin' for her,
    but this red-haired nester's brat
Admitted she had drawed it—
    so we both got licked for that!

Some years have drifted down the trail
    since them Red Canyon days.
I'm still a-punchin' cattle,
    so I ain't much changed my ways,
And Janie, she's the mother
    of a pair of red-haired kids
With pockets full of lizzards,
    toads and even katydids;
And one of them, or so I hear,
    got licked last week at school
For tyin' tin cans to the tail
    of some gal's ridin' mule.

So he's bought a fancy valentine,
  with crimson hearts and lace,
To give this gal for causin' her
  to get throwed on her face.
I'll bet she sure will like it—
  and her eyes will open wide
When she finds the ring-tailed lizzard
  he has hid for her inside!
I claim he gits his meanness
  from his pug-nosed, blue-eyed Ma.
My wife, she only kinder smiles and says:
  "Well, you're his Pa!"

I rode a buckskin pony
  and she rode a nester's mule—
And now we got two young'uns
  playin' monkeyshines at school.
I never will forget it—
  how her seat was next to mine . . . .
Her hair's as red as ever—
  and she's still my valentine!

Bedtime Story

She married a cowboy
  He keeps her awake
With sounds that are hard to excuse.
He's been around cows
So much that she vows
Instead of just snoring, he moos!

Wearin' Daddy's Hat

Through corral dust she can glimpse him,
    And she longs to call him in
For the men are bustin' broncos—
    But she knows his Dad will grin:

"Don't you fret about this young 'un!
    Let him stay right where he's at!
Ain't no bronco gonna stomp him
    While he's wearin' Daddy's hat!"

Ain't no bigger than a minute—
    Only seven, comin' spring—
But he's got his Daddy's hat on,
    And his rope is on the swing.

Struttin' like a banty rooster,
    Plumb hurrawin' ever' ride,
Same as any growed up cowhand—
    Plumb awares and eagle-eyed.

Big ol' hat that he could set in,
    Steppin' 'round and in the way—
But the hands, they kinder like him
    In that hat, and let him stay.

Got his Ma skeered to the gizzard,
    But his Dad—it tickles him,
Jest to see that young 'un struttin'
    Underneath that wide ol' brim.

Kinder dangerous? Yep, *she* knows it,
    But she's kinder proud, at that,
Seein' how he's like his Daddy
    When he's wearin' Daddy's hat.

Classic Rhymes by S. Omar Barker

The Ring-Tailed Wowser

They asked me "What's a wowser?'
    Well, a wowser is the critter
That the nester's little daughter
    is afraid will come and git her
In case she fails to wash her neck
    and mind her pa and ma,
For what the ring-tailed wowser
    likes is little gals to chaw.
At least she's heard the cowboys
    thus describe this wondrous beast
With one green eye a-lookin' west,
    a red one lookin' east.
But, speakin' scientifickly,
    the wowser is a cross
Between the cattywampus
    and the dry-land albatross,
With parts of grizzly bear throwed in,
    and just enough of 'coon
To give him rings around his tail,
    like rings around the moon.

His gran'pa was a cyclone
    like they have up Kansas way—,
His gran'ma was a minnywoo
    from Matagorda Bay.
He's cousin to the coyotes
    and akin to hooty owls
That's why he just don't give a hoot
    how wild he squalls and howls.
In color he's a bluish-pink,
    with spots of reddish-green.
Two purple stripes run down his back,
    which cactus grows between.

His horsehair mane is midnight black,
    and feathers from his head
Are plucked by Pecos Bill, I've heard,
    to stuff his Sunday bed.
His ears are rawhide hornet's nests
    some thirty-six feet wide.
The alkali on western flats
    is wowser slobbers, dried.
In size the wowser varies,
    for no matter where he's at,
He takes up all the room there is—
    just like a cowboy's hat.
His teeth are rusty staples
    that he steals from bobwire fence—
That's why maintainin' fences
    costs the cowman such expense.
He's built so squatty-legged
    that his feet don't reach the ground—
That's why you never find
    no tracks of wowsers layin' 'round.
What critter does he look like most?
    The best that I can do
Is to say that he resembles
    both the wup and minnywoo,
Which, though I've never seen 'em
    and I maybe never will,
Are pets just like the wowser
    on the ranch of Pecos Bill.
They asked me "What's a wowser?"
    One more line will get it skinned:
He's the cowboy's dream of dragons—
    and he's mostly made of wind!

Classic Rhymes by S. Omar Barker

Three Wise Men

Back in the days when cattle range
    was prairies wide and lone,
Three Bar Z hands was winter-camped
    upon the Cimarron.
Their callin' names was Booger Bill
    and Mexkin Pete and Tug,
And though their little dugout camp
    was plenty warm and snug,
They got plumb discontented;
    for with Christmas drawin' near,
They couldn't see no prospects
    of no kind of Christmas cheer.

Pete spoke about the *bailes*
    he'd be missin' up at Taos;
Tug said he'd give his gizzard
    just to see a human house
Alight with Christmas candles;
    and ol' Booger Bill avowed
He'd shoot the next galoot
    who spoke of Christmas cheer out loud!
They sure did have the lonesomes,
    but the first of Christmas week,
A wagon load of immigrants
    made camp off down the creek.

They'd come out from Missouri
    and was headin' further west,
But had to stop a little while
    and give their team a rest.
They seemed to be pore nester folks
    with maybe six or eight
As hungry lookin' barefoot kids
    as ever licked a plate.

"We've just got beans to offer you,"
    the wagon woman smiled,
"But if you boys will join us,
    I will have a big pot b'iled
On Christmas day for dinner,
    an' we'll do the best we kin
To make it seem like Christmas time,
    although our plates is tin!"

Them cowboys sort of stammered,
    but they promised her they'd come,
Then loped back to their dugout camp—
    and things begun to hum.
They whittled with their pocketknives,
    they sewed with rawhide threads,
They hammered and they braided
    and they raveled rope to shreds.
They butchered out a yearlin'
    and they baked a big ol' roast.
They scratched their heads to figger out
    what kids would like the most.

Till when they went on Christmas day
    to share the nesters' chuck,
They had a packhorse loaded
    with their home made Christmas truck.
Bandanna dolls for little gals,
    with raveled rope for hair;
Some whittled wooden guns for boys,
    and for each kid a pair
Of rough made rawhide moccasins.

Classic Rhymes by S. Omar Barker

You should have seen the look
Upon that nester woman's face
   when from their pack they took
A batch of pies plumb full of prunes,
   some taffy made of lick,
And a pan of sourdough biskits
   right around four inches thick!

That ain't the total tally,
   but it sort of gives a view
Of what three lonesome cowboys
   figgered out to try and do
To cure the Christmas lonesomes
   on the Cimarron amid
The wild coyotes and cattle—
   and they found it sure 'nough did!

Boy into Man

He's ridin' stick horses before he can walk,
  He's got a big hat by the time he can talk,
  And makes like a cowboy, the cute little dickens,
  By ropin' his puppy and cowboyin' chickens!

The first real ridin', of course, for the lad,
  Is safe in the arms of his cowpuncher dad,
  But then it ain't long till you'll purty sure find
  His short legs all spraddled out, ridin' behind,
  A-holdin' on tight to a belt or shirt tail,
  And giving all comers a buckaroo hail.

Before he is five, just as sure as you're born,
  He's ridin' alone, holdin' on to the horn,
  On some ol' tame pony they know they can trust,
  All swelled up with pride till he's purt near to bust!
  But although he's proud and his gizzard may swell,
  He's still just a button for quite a long spell.
  He's got to do chores and he's got to learn how
  To take to the fence from a snuffy ol' cow.

Classic Rhymes by S. Omar Barker

He's got to chop kindlin' and maybe pitch hay,
For ranch-working cowhands ain't made in a day.
He keeps on a-growin' and rides when he can,
A-countin' the months till he'll be a growed man.
He rides the colts bareback and takes a few falls,
But still has to answer his ma when she calls.

He's still just a kid. What they give him to ride
Is some ol' spare saddle that's been put aside,
Too wore out for cow-work. But some happy day
His prayers, will be answered. He'll hear his dad say,
"Well, son, here's a saddle. It's yours an' it's new.
Climb on it an' see if you think it'll do!"

From then on there ain't any horse he can't straddle,
For a ranch kid's a man when he gits his own saddle!

Ranch Mother

She knows the keen of lonely winds,
    The sound of hoofs at night,
    The creak of unwarmed saddles in
    The chill before daylight,
    The champ of eager bridle bits,
    The jingle-clink of spurs,
    The clump of boots—lone silence, too,
    For cowboy sons are hers.

    She knew the dust of cattle trails
    While yet she was a bride,
    And tangy smell of branding iron
    Upon a dogie's hide.
    The yelp of coyotes on a hill,
    The night hawk's lonely croon,
    The bawl of milling cattle: thus
    Her cowcamp honeymoon.

    Her hands are hard from laboring,
    Her face is brown from sun,
    But oh, her eyes are deep with dreams
    Of days and duties done!
    The hand of hardship forged her love
    That first far rangeland spring.
    Now he is gone its memory lives,
    A gentle, deathless thing.

    Her days knew little neighboring,
    Less now, perhaps, than then,
    Alone with years she gleans content:
    Her sons are horseback men!

Classic Rhymes by S. Omar Barker

Watchin' Em Ride

Isom Like was seventy-odd,
  Straight in the back as a steel ramrod,
  And the whiskers that growed on his leathery chin,
  They bristled out instead of in.
  Six growed sons had Isom Like:
  Jake, Joe, John, Jess, Noah and Ike.

Ridin' men was Isom's sons,
  Salty, straddlin' sons-o'-guns.
  Once a year they chipped in change
  To pay for the best hoss on their range,
  And held a ridin' to settle who
  Should git that hoss when the show was through.

Nearin' eighty was Isom Like:
  "Pa," said the son whose name was Ike,
  "You're stiffed up like an ol' pine tree.
  Better leave this to the boys an' me!"
  Ol' Isom grinned his grizzled grin.
  "Nope," he says. "Just count me in!"

Seven broncs in a high pole pen,
  Seven saddles and seven men . . . .
  Ma Like watched as the show begun,
  And when Jake straddled a dusty dun,
  You guessed right off that her joy and pride
  Was Jake, from the way she cheered his ride.

Jess spurred out on a big-foot bay.
  Up on the fence you could hear Ma say:
  "Ride him, Jess! Boy, kick him out!"
  And you knowed right quick from the tone of her shout,
  Of all six sons Ma Like had bore,
  By this here Jess she set most store.

Joe clumb on and you heard Ma squall:
"Joe, you're the ridin'est son of all!"
Noah an' John purt near got piled—
But both was Ma Like's favorite child.
Two broncs left, and the one Ike took
Bucked like the broncs in a storybook;
Pawed the moon and scraped the sky.
Up on the fence you could hear Ma cry:
"Boy, that's ridin' to suit my taste!
I got one son ain't no panty-waist!"

One bronc left, a big blue roan . . . .
"Never mind, boys, I'll saddle my own!"
Over the saddle Pa flung his shank,
Raked both spurs from neck to flank.
The big roan rose like a powder blast,
Buckin' hard and high and fast,
But deep in the wood Pa Like set screwed,
Strokin' his beard like a southern dude!
And every time that blue roan whirled,
Ma Like's petticoats come unfurled.

Isom grinned and waved his hat,
And Ma, she squalled like a ring-tailed cat:
"Straddle him, Isom! Show your spizz!
Learn these buttons what ridin' is!"
Throwed her bonnet high in the air,
Whooped and hollered and tore her hair:
"I got six sons and nary a one
Can ride like that ol' son-of-a-gun!"
Yelled and cheered so dang intense
She fell plumb off of the high pole fence.
"Wawhoo, boys! Watch Isom spur!"
Isom's six sons grinned at her.

Classic Rhymes by S. Omar Barker

Seven broncs and the ridin' done . . . .
Nary a doubt but Pa had won!
"Sons," says Ma, "are a mother's pride,
But ol' Pa Isom, *he can ride!*
The trouble is, you boys ain't tough—
But you'll learn to *ride—when you're old enough!*"

(Based on a true incident related by the late Col. Jack Potter. Isom Like died at the age of 102.)

Ranchman's Widow

She's got one son a doctor,
   And a daughter teachin' Latin.
Her youngest, he's a lawyer,
   And she thinks a heap of that 'un,
But one's a cow ranch foreman,
   And it makes her kinder glad,
For the way he set the saddle
   Just reminds her of his dad.

She's proud to be the mother
   Of a man who tends the sick,
And of a brainy daughter,
   And a lawyer, keen and quick;
But when her old heart hankers
   For the old days once again,
She packs and makes a visit
   To the range of ridin' men.

And although he aint ambitious
   For a big high-toned success,
Her cowboy son arouses
   Just a heap more tenderness.
Than all the other trio,
   And her heart feels young and glad
Just to see him set the saddle
   Like his old cowpuncher dad.

Classic Rhymes by S. Omar Barker

Curly Wolf College

I went up to a college and they asked me what I knowed
 To justify embarkin' on the education road.
I told 'em that my Pa and Ma had figgered I was smart,
For I could purt near always tell a horse and cow apart:
A cow's the one that wears the horns, a horse is what you ride,
And both of them most always wears the hairy part outside.

They asked me what I knowed about the hist'ry of the earth.
I told 'em that I understood it started at Fort Worth,
Where Adam, the first Texan, found a market for his steers,
And started raisin' buckaroos with red and hairy ears.
They asked about my algebra—I told 'em it was tough,
The way most any cowboy's gits that's ridden long enough.

They asked me what philosophy of life I favored most,
And that one sure did snub me right up to the snubbin' post.
I pondered some, then told 'em that I always do my best
To aim my spittin' eastwards when the wind is in the west.
They asked about my grammar, and I told 'em she was dead.
They didn't mention Grampa, but I told 'em what he'd said:
That any man was foolish and was shorely bound to fail
Who'd kick a hog barefooted or twist a panther's tail!

I went up to this college, but I didn't stay there long,
For they asked a heap of questions and my answers was all wrong.
At least that's how *they* figgered, like them college fellers do,
But I brought a prof back with me just to spend a week or two
A-ridin' on the rancho with a hoss between his knees,
Where the wolves is wild an' curly and the kiotes all got fleas.

About this here perfessor I won't say no word unkind,
For he packs a heap of knowledge in that thing he calls his mind;
But now *my* lack of learnin' don't seem near so woebegone—
At least *I* know which end to put the horse's bridle on!

Mountain Ranch Wife

Gray twilight deepens into dusk
    Dark shadows blur rail fence and gates,
    Cool comes the jack-pines fragrant musk
    Upon the breeze . . . . She waits.

    She waits alone, her ears one ache
    Of listening for the welcome sound
    His coming down the trail should make,
    Of spurs or hoofs against the ground.

    He rode away when dawn was dim.
    Those high range trails are danger filled.
    What if that new bronc fell with him?
    Suppose . . . . He could be killed!

    Gray shadows blacken into night,
    Before the door a bullbat whirs,
    Moths flicker in her yellow light—
    And still no comforting is hers.

    The clock ticks on, a hill breeze blows.
    Suddenly, softly, out at the gate,
    The sweetest music a ranch wife knows:
    The jingle of spurs when he comes in late!

Classic Rhymes by S. Omar Barker

A Frontier Wife

She saw them crawling, closing in,
   And in her cabin door,
She raised the shotgun to her chin—
Their leader crawled no more.
Apaches—and her husband gone,
   One hired man to help!
Blood-chilling through the dusty dawn
She heard the Indians yelp.

Now like hard hail the bullets came
   To crash the window through.
She stood and answered with the same,
As any man would do.
Three times the yelling reds' attack
   Was quelled by shot and ball.
She saw the savages come back,
The man beside her fall.

The hours dragged, and still she kept
   The savage pack at bay,
Till o'er the hill ten cowboys swept,
And drove the reds away.
They said they'd send her husband word.
   She answered like a man:
"He's gone to town to ship a herd.
He'll get back when he can.

But take a message, if you will—
The first who's going down—
A little order he can fill
And send it out from town."
Then Mrs. Stevens took her pen
And penned a little note.

The easy years have come since then . . .
But this is what she wrote:
"Dear Lewis: All is quiet here.
There's been some reds about.
You'd better send some buckshot, dear
I've just about run out."

Ranch House Night

An ol' cow bawlin' down the draw,
  A windmill's lonesome whirr,
Are sounds as sweet to cowfolks
  As a kitten's cozy purr.

The Cowgirl at College

Oh, the grass on the range of the old Bar G
    Is turning a winter gray,
Where the fat herds graze contentedly—
    And I so far away!

There is a crispy tang from the sage to smell
    And a smack of frost in the wind,
But I must hark to a college bell
    That calls to the classroom grind.

Through eyes half closed I can glimpse the blue
    Of haze on Cacho Peak—
I open them and stare into
    A brand book full of Greek!

The sound of creaking saddles sings,
    And jingle-song of spurs—
With west wind wants and visioning
    My lonely being stirs.

His First Shave

"Too young to straddle broncs, my lad!
    You're just a beardless sprout!
My broncs are mighty mean and bad.
    They'd spill you on your snout!"
So spoke the Bar L's grizzled boss.
    The Kid said: "Shucks! Who's skeered?
Who ever rode a buckin' hoss
    That held on by his beard?"

"Too young to guard a herd by night
    You're just sixteen and show it."
The Kid said: "Shucks! I'm young all right,
    But do them cattle know it?"
"This posse's job is too dang tough.
    You wait until you're bigger!"
"Aw shucks! My finger's big enough
    To pull a sixgun trigger!"

Too young? Brave Cap McNelly's men,
    Of Texas Ranger fame,
Who smoked King Fisher from his den
    Were aged about the same.
The Bar L boss said: "Stay behind!"
    The posse rode away.
The fuzz-faced Kid made up his mind:
    "I'll foller anyway!"
Hard rode the posse, day and night,
    Upon the rustlers' trail,
And swift behind them, out of sight,
    The Kid loped at their tail.

An ambush in a canyon's rift,
    The posse trapped, at bay.
The Kid came on. His shots were swift
    To save their lives that day.
That night the boss grinned wide and free:
    "Twas man-style lead you throwed!
If that's kid stuff, you'll surely be
    A bearcat when you're growed!"
The Kid said: "Shucks! I'm just sixteen!
    Just somehow can't behave!
Who's got a razor nice and keen?
    I think I need a shave!"

Cowpuncher Praise

Big words never warm up a cowpuncher's heart
    In praise of him doin' his best,
Like one simple phrase. A man does his part—
    "He'll do, boys!" they say in the West.

Ravens Over the Pass

Riderless came the horse to camp
    When the wild plums were in bud,
And the cowboys found the saddle damp
    With a drying smear of blood!
A riderless horse is a woeful thing,
    Wandering in alone,
Dragging his reins, on a day in spring,
    And the rider's name unknown.

"I'll ride the track," the straw boss said.
    "You boys sweep wide for sign.
Watch out for ravens overhead.
    That horse brand once was mine."
The straw boss was a gray-haired man
    With distance in his eyes,
Of saddle and trail a veteran,
    Schooled by the open skies.

He rode a high ridge to the west,
    And the roan's back track was clear.
Two cawing ravens left their nest
    To shadow him with fear.
Not fear of body, but a strange
    Unfathomed fear of mind,
Born of his own past on the range,
    Dreading what he might find.

Somewhere far toward the sunset's flame,
    Once he had had a son,
But now he lived by another name,
    Thanks to a deed long done.
The straw boss rode where the ravens led,
    Until in a narrow pass,
He found a black-haired cowboy dead,
    And blood upon the grass.

The sheriff rode up with gun at hip.
    His words used little breath:
"This horsethief gave my men the slip,
    And him done shot to death!"
The straw boss gazed down at the boy
    Who'd ridden here to die,
And in his heart there was no joy,
    Nor comfort in his eye.

For a riderless horse is a woeful thing,
    Wandering in alone,
Dragging his reins on a day in spring,
    His rider's name unknown.

Holidays

Classic Rhymes by S. Omar Barker

Bunkhouse Thanksgiving

A beef roast in the oven
    and the hands all waitin' 'round,
So they got to kinder talkin' 'bout
    the different things they'd found
That each of them was thankful for
    on this Thanksgiving Day,
And some, they told it solemn-like,
    and some, they told it gay.

Tom thanked the Lord
    that hosses had four legs instead of two,
So cowboys didn't have to walk
    like some poor suckers do.
Ol' Bashful claimed
    that women was the blessing in his life—
No doubt he meant his mother,
    for he'll never git a wife!

"I'm thankful most for cattle, boys,"
    says Slim, who thinks a heap.
"In a world without them critters
    we would all be herdin' sheep!"
The Ramrod spoke his thankfulness
    that grass was good and long,
And Curly said he thanked the stars
    that he was young and strong,
While Bud, he blessed his appetite.
    The way that beef roast smelt,
He also felt thanksgivin'
    for the long holes in his belt!

Ol' Dunk, he kinder sucked his pipe
    and gazed off toward the hills.
"Well, boys," he says,
    "I'm sixty-five and full of liver pills.
My rheumatism aches me
    and my pipe is gittin' stale.
My hossy days are over,
    and I'm feelin' purty pale.
My bunion's grown so bulbous
    that I've had to split my boot.
My ears—I'd have to climb the tree
    to hear a hoot owl hoot.
Cain't down my woes in likker,
    for my ticker's on the blink.
I cain't enjoy the cattylogs,
    the way my blinkers wink.
I've got some nose for smellin' left—
    that roast is purt near done,
But all the chawin' teeth I've got
    adds up to only one.
Ol' Gus shore savvies cookin' beef!
    I'd like to eat a pound,
But hell, I couldn't chaw it
    if he took and had it ground!

"You talk about Thanksgivin', boys,
    and here you see me set,
A plumb wore-out ol' cowhand—
    but I'm mighty thankful yet
For every hoss I've ever rode
    and every sight I've saw,
But most of all for gravy—
    which a man don't have to chaw!"

Classic Rhymes by S. Omar Barker

Drifter's Thanksgivin'

Away out West long years ago,
    It came Thanksgivin' time,
And caught this cowboy busted flat.
    He didn't have a dime,
Nor nothin' else to speak of
    But a hungry appetite;
No turkey dinner 'neath his belt,
    No place to spend the night.
The day was raw and chilly
    And the afternoon was late.
The wore-out hoss he rode upon
    Was purt near buzzard-bait.

A drifter huntin' him a job,
    With nothin' turnin' up,
He rode this stretch of desert
    Like a lost and lonesome pup,
A-thinkin' surely purty soon
    Some ranch would come in view.,
With dinner on the table
    That they might invite him to.
But all he saw was prairie dogs,
    As mile on mile he rode,
With here and there a rabbit
    Or an ugly horny toad.
No human habitation,
    Nary ranch house, nary shack,
Until he felt his stummick
    Rubbin' plumb against his back.

Then all at once a dugout's door
    Stood open in the gloom,
And in it stood a cowboy,
    Bristlin' whiskers like a broom.
"Light down! Light down!" this cowboy says.
    "I'm settin' supper out—
Except in case you don't like beans,
    You'll have to do without
For this here is a line-camp
    That's so doggoned far from taw
That the boss ain't sent no vittles out
    Since Jacob fooled his Pa!"

A candle lit the boar's nest
    When them two set down to bread,
A pot of beans, and coffee.
    Then this drifter bowed his bead.
"O Lord," he says, "up yonder
    Where the well-fed angels dwell,
Since this here is the day for thanks,
    Seems like I might as well
Cut loose and say a word or two
    About this bill of fare.

Classic Rhymes by S. Omar Barker

When I had cash I spent it
   Like a Klondike millionaire.
You take Thanksgivin' last year—
   Well, I fed on turkey breast,
Cranberry sauce and gravy—
   Which is what I like the best.
But I forgot to thank YOU, Lord,
   When luck was runnin' good,
So now I'm settin' down to beans,
   I sorter thought I would.
The pot looks kinder skimpy,
   But I'm thankful in my heart
That You and this kind stranger
   Aim to let me eat my part.

Thanksgivin' Day is somethin'
   That a man can understand
When he's got an empty stummick
   Underneath his bellyband.
And so tonight I thank You,
   Lord of North, South, West and East,
For learnin' me the lesson
   That plain beans can be a feast!"

Thanksgiving Argument

About this here Thanksgiving
    there are two opposin' views,
One helt by ol' Pop McIntyre,
    one helt by Smoky Hughes;
And how them two ol' cowpokes
    will debate the pros-and-cons
Produces in the bunkhouse
    many verbal marathons.
"I've always worked," says Smoky,
    "for whatever I have had,
Since first I wrangled horses
    as a rusty-knuckled lad.
I've rode my share of broncos,
    and I've punched a heap of cow,
And earned my own danged 'blessings'
    by the sweat of my own brow!
Why I should be a-givin' thanks
    for what I've duly earned
Is a lot of bosh and bunkum
    that I just ain't never learned!"

Pop McIntyre, he sucks his pipe
    a thoughtful draw or two,
Then says: "Well, Smoky,
    I'll admit that you're a buckaroo
Who sets a steady saddle
    and ain't stingy with his sweat,
But maybe there's a thing or two
    you stubbornly forget.
You're noted as a peeler
    that is seldom ever throwed—
To what good luck or blessin'
    is your skill at ridin' owed?"

Classic Rhymes by S. Omar Barker

"There ain't no good luck to it, Pop,"
    says Smoky. "I'm a man
Who ain't obliged for nothin'
    when I do the best I can.
For when I earn my wages
    bustin' out a bunch of colts,
It's me, myself in person,
    that is takin' all the jolts.
That's why I claim Thanksgivin' Day
    is mostly just a fake
To give some folks a good excuse
    for turkey stummick-ache!"

"My friend," says Pop, sarcastic,
    "you have spoke your little piece,
And proved you've got a limber tongue
    that's well supplied with grease.
You scoff at all thanksgivin',
    but a fact you surely know
Is that some Power beyond your own
    learned blades of grass to grow.
You spoke of ridin' broncos—
    I'll admit you ride 'em good,
And set up in the saddle
    like a salty peeler should.
For this you take the credit,
    and you claim to owe no thanks
For the buckarooster blessin'
    of the muscles in your shanks!
Instead you should feel thankful,"
    says Pop's concludin' drawl,
"That the good Lord made you forked—
    or you couldn't ride *at all!*"

Draggin' in the Tree

The cowboy ain't no lumberjack,
    an' if you want the facks,
One thing he ain't the fondest of
    is choppin' with an axe
But when December snow has got the range
    all wrapped in white,
There is one job of choppin'
    that he seems to like all right.
A sharp ax on his shoulder,
    he will ride off up the draw
Until he finds an evergreen
    without a single flaw.
A spruce, a fir, a juniper
    that's shaped just to a T
To set up in a corner
    for the ranchhouse Christmas tree.

As like as not, last summer
    while a-ridin' after cows
He noticed just the tree he wants,
    with green an' graceful boughs
That's stout enough to ornament
    without no droop nor saggin',
But still a tree that ain't too big
    to fetch without a wagon.
It may be that he picked it out
    when August sun was hot,
But he knows where to find it,
    for his mind has marked the spot.

It ain't no chore to chop it down,
    an' if the snow is deep,
He drags it in behind his horse.
    It warms him up a heap
To see them rancher kids
    run out a-hollerin' with glee
To watch him an' admire him
    when he's bringin' the tree.

Them kids may not belong to him,
    but that don't matter none—
His boss' brood, a nesters brats—
    It's still a heap of fun
To some ol' lonesome cowpoke,
    an' it sets his heart aglow
To come a-draggin' in the tree
    across the Christmas snow.
Sometimes when there's a schoolmarm
    an' she wants a tree at school,
She gets half a dozen,
    for you'll find that as a rule
At least that many cowboys,
    in sweet educaton's cause,
Will somehow get to feelin'
    that they're kin to Santy Claus!

Sometimes the rangeland's lonesome
    an' sometimes it's kind o' grim,
But not when every ranchhouse
    has a Christmas tree to trim.
An' though the wild cowpuncher
    ain't no hand to swing an ax,
Across the white December snow
    you'll often find his tracks
A-leadin' to the timber,
    then back out again once more,
A-draggin' in the Christmas tree—
    his purt near favorite chore!

Line-Camp Christmas Letter

Inside an Old West line-camp,
    settin' on his lonely bed,
A cowboy wrote a letter home,
    and this is what it said:
"Dear Folks: It looks like Christmas time
    is comin' on again,
And I ain't wrote no letter
    since the devil don't know when.

So now I thought I'd drop a line
    just like I done last year,
To let you know I'm safe and well
    and full of Christmas cheer.
Seems like the news ain't much to tell.
    A blizzard blowin' now.
There'll be some cattle driftin'.
    Merry Christmas anyhow!

I've been out ridin' most all day.
    The horse I rode went lame.
The cattle sure are scattered.
    Merry Christmas just the same!
Last night my waterholes froze up.
    Snow sure is slow to thaw.
Some cattle lookin' porely.
    Merry Christmas, Pa and Ma!

Classic Rhymes by S. Omar Barker

This line-camp shack has got some cracks
    that let the snow sift through.
Well, Merry Christmas to you, folks,
    and Happy New Year, too!
Excuse this crooked writin'.
    Got my hands frostbite I guess.
The cattle sure are driftin'.
    Merry Christmas, Frank and Bes!

Ax handle busted. Woodpile low.
    Ain't got much fire tonight.
The drifts have knocked some line fence down.
    I trust you're all all right.
My pot of beans boiled dry
    and scorched while I was out today.
Them cows are driftin' awful.
    Merry Christmas anyway!

Well, folks, I've got to cut this short
    and mend my busted rope.
Just thought I'd drop a little line.
    You all keep well, I hope.
This cowboy life is wonderful.
    Sure glad I came out West.
Give my regards to Adelaide
    and Jack and all the rest.
I'm glad I ain't a cow tonight.
    Outside I hear 'em bawl.
Pore critters sure are driftin'.
    Merry Christmas to you all!"

A Cowboy's Christmas Prayer

I ain't much good at prayin',
    and You may not know me, Lord—
I ain't much seen in churches
    where they preach Thy Holy Word,
But You may have observed me
    out here on the lonely plains,
A-lookin' after cattle,
    feelin' thankful when it rains,

Admirin' Thy great handiwork,
    the miracle of grass,
Aware of Thy kind spirit
    in the way it comes to pass
That hired men on horseback
    and the livestock that we tend
Can look up at the stars at night
    and know we've got a Friend.

So here's ol' Christmas comin' on,
    remindin' us again
Of Him whose coming brought good will
    into the hearts of men.

Classic Rhymes by S. Omar Barker

A cowboy ain't a preacher, Lord,
    but if You'll hear my prayer,
I'll ask as good as we have got
    for all men everywhere.

Don't let no hearts be bitter, Lord.
    Don't let no child be cold.
Make easy beds for them that's sick
    and them that's weak and old.
Let kindness bless the trail we ride,
    no matter what we're after,
And sorter keep us on Your side,
    in tears as well as laughter.

I've seen ol' cows a-starvin',
    and it ain't no happy sight:
Please don't leave no one hungry, Lord,
    on Thy good Christmas night—
No man, no child, no woman,
    and no critter on four feet
I'll do my doggone best
    to help you find 'em chuck to eat.

I'm just a sinful cowpoke, Lord—
    ain't got no business prayin'
But still I hope you'll ketch a word
    or two of what I'm sayin:
We speak of Merry Christmas, Lord—
    I reckon You'll agree—

There ain't no Merry Christmas
    for nobody that ain't free!
So one thing more I'll ask You,
    Lord: just help us what You can
To save some seeds of freedom
    for the future sons of man!

The Cowboy's Religion

Oh, churches and preachin' and singin' of hymns
    Is fine for the city people,
But ridin' the range on the mesas' rims
    I never see nary a steeple.

I ain't been to church since old Leatherwood died,
    But I ain't ashamed to admit it,
Fer I've got religion deep under my hide,
    And this is the way I git it:

Just bein' a man and a-lopin' along
    Where the world is like God made it,
And sometimes at night, with a bit of a song,
    A-tryin' to serenade it.

The hills are my friends and the prairie's my pal,
    The stars are my next door neighbors—
My kind of believin' ain't schismatical,
    Nor somethin' apart from my labors.

Fer out on the ranges of square-shootin' men
    Us boys never hears much preachin'—
I reckon God hears us a-worshipin' when
    We follow His Nature's teachin'.

Drylander's Christmas

Four days before Christmas out on the Bar U
A case of the lonesomes had hit the whole crew.
Though mostly young fellers who'd drifted out West
Plumb off from their homefolks, it must be confessed
That comin' on Christmas, them lonesomes took hold.
As the dadblasted weather tuned stormy and cold.
With the trail snowed too deep for a town gallyhoot.
Their chances for Christmas cheer weren't worth a hoot.
There'd be stock to tend to—some strays like as not—
And not much for Christmas but beans in a pot.

Now family homes in them days long ago
Was scattered plum thin and as old-timer's know
The feelin's 'twixt nesters and range-ridin' men
Was often plumb hostile. So here it had been
Till just before Christmas homesteader O'Toole
Took a notion that he'd put a boy on a mule
To spread the good word that on Christmas Eve night
His house would be warm, and with candles alight,
His missus and him would both welcome that crew
Of snowbounded cowhands out on the Bar U.
They said there'd be fixin's and maybe a chance
There might be some music and maybe some dance.

So the cowboys rode over in spite of the snow,
With the mercury hangin' about ten below.
Another farm family from off up the draw
Showed up in a wagon, not just pa and ma
But also three daughters. Believe it or not,
On that Christmas Eve all feuds was forgot!
And in that snug house on the drylander's claim
Five frostbitten cowhands were sure glad they came.
For the best Merry Christmas, them buckaroos found,
Is always the one where there's women around;
And if you ain't guessed it, 'twas *Missus* O'Toole
Who'd made the old man put that boy on a mule!

Cowboy's New Year's Resolutions

As one who's been a cowhand
　　since the wildcats learned to spit,
I've made some resolutions
　　for the comin' year, to wit:
Resolved, to ride a shorter day
　　and sleep a longer night;
To never come to breakfast
　　till the sun is shinin' bright;
To draw a top-hand's wages
　　when they're due or quit the job
And hunt a wealthy widow
　　or an easy bank to rob.
Resolved, to quit the wagon
　　when the chuck ain't up to snuff,
To feed no more on bullet beans
　　nor chaw no beef that's tough.
Resolved, to straddle
　　nothin' in the line of saddle mount
That ain't plumb easy-gaited,
　　gentle broke, and some account.

Resolved, that when it blizzards
　　and there's stock out in the storm,
To let the owner worry
　　while I stay in where it's warm.
Resolved, that when it comes
　　my turn next spring to ride the bogs,
I'll don the bib and tucker
　　of my town and Sunday togs,
And tell the boss, by gravies,
　　if he craves to shed some blood,
Just try to make me smear 'em
　　tailin' moo-cows from the mud.

Resolved, that when a thunderhead
    comes rollin' up the sky,
I'll lope in off my circle
    to the bunkhouse where it's dry.

Resolved, to do such ropin'
    as a ropin' cowhand must,
But never when the air ain't free
    from cattle-trompled dust.
Resolved, to shoe no hosses,
    and resolved, to swim no cricks;
Resolved, no dead-cow skinnin',
    and resolved, no fence to fix.
Resolved, to swing no pitchfork,
    no pick, no ax, no spade;
Resolved, to wear my whiskers—
    if I want to—in a braid!
Resolved, to take this New Year
    plenty easy through-and-through,
Instead of sweatin' heavy like
    I've always used to do.

As one who's been a cowhand
    since before who laid the chunk,
It may sound like I'm *loco*,
    or it may sound like I'm drunk
To make such resolutions
    as you see upon my list,
And others purt near like 'em
    that my mem'ry may have missed;

But gosh, they sound so pleasant
    to a son of saddle sweat!
And New Year's resolutions—
    well, I never kept one yet!
So why make resolutions
    that bring furrows to your brow?
Let's make 'em free and fancy—'
    cause we'll bust 'em anyhow!

Ranch Life

Cow Country

Here is a country still unplowed,
    Where untamed grasses lift
    Their heads on mesas rimrock-browed,
    In canyons steeply cliffed.

    Here is a land that knows the pain
    Of drought and drying sod,
    Yet greens again each time that rain
    Renews its faith in God.

    It is a proud and patient land,
    Possessed and understood
    By men as sunburnt as its sand,
    Who love and find it good.

The Chuckwagon

They asked me: "What's this wagon
    that we hear so much about.
Aren't wagons simply wagons?"
    Well, it kinder laid me out
To realize such ignorance
    was still a-runnin' rife
About cow country customs
    and the facts of cowboy life.

And so I found a sunny place
    and squatted on my heels
To try and make them savvy
    that a double pair of wheels
Ain't all that makes the wagon,
    in the meanin' of the word,
The way us cowboys use it
    that have been out with a herd.

For a wagon ain't The Wagon
    on the roundup or the trail
Unless it totes a chuckbox
    handy-like upon its tail.
This chuckbox is the cupboard
    where the coosie keeps the gear
With which he wrangles rations
    for the cowboy cavalier

Who comes in off the cow work,
    like a farmer to his shack,
To save his hungry stummick
    from a-growin' to his back.
He may git whistle-berries
    and shotgun-waddin' bread,
It may be beef and biskits,
    but it gits the cowhand fed.

Yet chuck ain't all The Wagon means
    to sons of saddle sweat.
It means dry clothes, a bed, a fire,
    and somewhere he can set
To do what little talkin'
    that the cowboy's life allows
About the thoughts he's thinkin'
    while he's out there with the cows.
It's where his comrades bring him
    when he's sick or hurt or shot;
It's his anchor, it's his haven,
    it's the only home he's got.
So when he throws his bedroll in
    The Wagon for a "work,"
It means he's swore allegiance
    to a job he'll never shirk.
You've heard of soldiers loyal
    to the flags of regiments—
The cowhand's flag's The Wagon
    and the brand it represents.

They asked me: "What's The Wagon?"
    It's, a thing words can't explain,
Unless you've bedded 'round one,
    under stars out on the plain.
Two lonesome riders passin'
    pause to hail, like passin' ships,
And 'Whichaways The Wagon?"
    Is the question on their lips.
So when a cowboy's time has come,
    St. Peter hears his hail:
It's "Whichaways The Wagon?" . . .
    And he points him up the trail!

Black Magic

He may feed you fried sow boozem
   Till you're sweatin' pure lard,
   But if he's got the java hot
   When you come in from guard,
   So you can swig a blister cup
   To ease you from the cold,
   You'll claim you've got a wagon cook
   That's worth his weight in gold.

   For puddin' let him kinder bog
   Some raisins in some dough,
   Or feed you "Texas butter"
   Till you swaller kinder slow,
   But if the beans are meller
   In his whistle-berry pot,
   And the coffee's always ready,
   And it's black and steamin' hot,
   You can stand a little ashes
   In the sop or in the dip,
   And the gun you use for shootin' cooks
   Will stay right on your hip.

He'll flap you "saddle blankets"
Tough enough to line a kack,
And mix a "hossthief special"
That will bulge you front and back,
Put sody in the biskits
Till your skin's a yaller hue,
Or leave the horns and hide on
When be cooks a maverick stew.
But still you'll meekly eat his chuck
And never fire a shot,
If, when you play the java pot,
It's *always* black and hot.
For a coosie at the wagon,
He can always hit the spot,
And he ain't no belly-cheater
If *he keeps the coffee hot!*

Buckaroo's Coffee

Now here is the recipe, time-tried and true,
  For chuck wagon coffee, the buckaroo's brew:
  Use Arbuckle's Roasted, in case you can get it;
  Pour in enough water to just sort of wet it.
  Boil hard for an hour, then into it toss
  The well rusted shoe off a clubfooted hoss;
  Gaze into the pot for a few minutes steady—
  If the hoss shoe is floating, your coffee is ready!

Hot Ir'n!

The thumpin' sound o' hosses' hoofs,
    The clack o' runnin' cows,
The song o' loopin' lassos on the swing,
The smell o' cedar fire,
    An' then to make yer pulses rouse,
Yuh hear some cowboy beller forth an' sing:
        "Hot ir'n! Hot ir'n!
      Wup! Come on, snap it up!
          Hot ir'n!'

Yuh grab the red irons from the fire
    An' run to where he's downed
A bawlin' calf an' holds him with his loop;
Yuh slap 'em on the hairy hide.
    The Ma cow bellers round
An' makes a bluff at hookin' where yuh stoop.
        "Hot ir'n! Hot ir'n!
      Come, burn 'em 'Rafter Bell'!
        Hey! Bring 'em hot as hell!
          Hot ir'n!"

Classic Rhymes by S. Omar Barker

All day the ropers drag the calves
    From out the millin' herd,
All day there's dust an' stink o' singein' hair!
The noise kinder makes yer ears buzz
    Like a hummin' bird—
Then rancous-squawkus hollers split the air:
    "Hot ir'n! Hot ir'n!
    Cain't hold this calf all day!
    Come on! Hey, what yuh say?
        Hot ir'n!"

It ain't the sweetest kind o' work—
    Calf brandin' on the range—
It's lots o' labor, dirt an' burnt hair smell,
But still I ain't a-hankerin'
    To see the old ways change,
I kinder like to hear that raspin' yell:

    "Hot ir'n! Hot ir'n!
    This dogie here I've got
    He'll git up like as not!
    Hey, cowboy! Bring 'em HOT!
      HOT' IR'N!"

Quittin' Talk

When it gits to stormin' on the trail—
    them spells of dismal rain—
The herd gits mighty snuffy,
    an' the hands, they git profane.
The cowchips all git stinkin' wet,
    the cook cain't rouse no fire;
You waller in your bedroll
    like a boar-hawg in the mire;
There ain't no coffee steamin'
    when you slog in from your guard,
You start to cuss the coosie,
    when you feel the whole earth jarred,
An' know the herd has spooked ag'in
    An' all you've got to do
Is grab your hoss an' ride it out
    until the run is through.

So dark your fingers can't find your face
    to scratch your nose,
It's slushy in your saddle seat
    an' squishy in your clothes.
There's dogholes an' arroyos
    even out upon the plains,
An' hell ain't far from Texas,
    with death reachin' for the reins.
You may ride through to daylight,
    but you don't know where you're at.
For there ain't no sun to go by
    an' it's foggy on the flat.
You've rode the legs plumb off your horse—
    you won't git off an' walk.
At last you find the wagon
    an' you make some salty talk.

You swear by all that's hairy
    that when this here drive is o'er,
You're trailin' days is finished
    an' you'll never ride no more.
You bow your neck an' beller
    an' you sure do paw the ground;
The Boss jest keeps his shirt on,
    for he's kinder been around
An' he knows the cowboy's quittin' talk
    from A plumb down to Z
Is like a dog that growls a heap
    but wouldn't bite a flea.

For when it's been a-stormin'
    an' you've rode a bad stampede,
A cowboy does some cussin'—
    which they don't nobody heed;
Because, when once it's over
    an' the herd is trailin' swell,
You know the Boss could spare you,
    but you wouldn't quit for hell!
It's when You're wet an' hungry
    an' the goin's mighty tough,
You make big talk of quittin',
    an' it sure ain't meant for bluff.
But you won't quit when it's easy
    An' you know damn well you can,
An' you don't quit when you're needed—
    for you ain't that breed of man!

Bear Ropin' Buckaroo

Now ropin' bears (says Uncle Sid)
    is sure a heap of fun,
And a lot more gizzard-thrillin'
    than to shoot 'em with a gun.
I roped a big ol' he one time
    when I was young and raw.
He must have weighed five hundred pounds,
    and monstrous was his paw.
He'd wandered out upon the flats
    for cowchip bugs and such.
Them grubs and worms,
    they suit a bear like pretzels suit the Dutch.
I purt near didn't ketch him,
    for a bear can split the breeze,
And your pony's got to wiggle
    if he beats him to the trees.
But the roan that I was ridin',
    he was tough and mighty fleet.
He overhauled ol' bruin,
    and my loop was quick and neat.
It ketched him snug around the neck,
    and when he hit the end,
I heard the cinches stretchin',
    and I felt the saddle bend!
My pony put the brakes on
    till he sure 'nough plowed the ground.
It purt near made me sorry
    that there weren't no crowd around
To watch a salty hand like me
    demonstrate my skill
At learnin' Mister Bruin
    to obey my wish and will!

"Come on, ol' b'ar!" I bellered.
   "You're a wild and woolly scamp,
But I'm the apparatus
   that can lead you into camp!"
At first I feared the rope would bust.
   I'd lose him if it should.
About a minute later, boys,
   I wished to hell it would!
That bear r'ared up and popped his teeth—
   'twas like a pistol crack—
Then grabbed my rope hand over hand
   and come right up the slack.

I gave a squall and swung my hat
   to slap him in the eyes,
But a he-bear ain't a critter
   that it's easy to surprise.
My pony tried to quit me,
   but he had a bear in tow,
And a-clingin' to the saddle
   was a load he couldn't throw.
He got a-straddle of the rope,
   a log, a bush, a bear.
He wallered on his haunches,
   and he pawed the upper air.
Ol' bruin's jaws and paws and claws,
   they purt had me skun.
My rope was anchored to the horn
   and wouldn't come undone.
Seemed like we fought for hours,
   and I couldn't see no hope,
When bruin bit my twine in two
   and quit us on the lope.

Now ropin' bears (says Uncle Sid)
    Is sure a heap of fun.
At least I've heard folks claim it is—
    I never roped but one.
It ain't no special trick at all
    to snag one in your noose.
The ketch is mighty simple—
    but it's hell to turn him loose!

Fireside Windies

Now cowboys 'round the fire at night,
    They tell it wide and high
Of broncs they've rode and gals they've kissed
    In other days gone by.
Till by the time the fire goes down,
    And all hands hit the straw,
They've rode more broncs and kissed more gals
    Than a cowboy ever saw!

Classic Rhymes by S. Omar Barker

Boar's Nest Batcher

I'm holdin' down the Boar's Nest,
    and a cookin' fer myself;
A chunk of sow hangs frum a nail,
    the lick can's on the shelf.
The prunes is shriveled up so hard
    they take two days to boil.
I'm outa bakin' powders
    and I'm outa lantern oil.

My coffee pot has sprung a leak;
    the gravy that I make
Would float a two pound biskit,
    and my pepper can won't shake.
The bootjack sets beside the bunk
    I ain't made up in weeks,
And whiskers thick as grammer grass
    adorns my manly cheeks.

I set on beans at sun-up,
    with a hot fire in the grate—
I dish 'em out for supper,
    and they rattle in the plate.
I've studied through four catalogs,
    wore out three almanacks,
Till knowledge bulges out my ears
    about them kind of facks.

By day I doctor screw worms,
    and I ride the lonely bogs;
By night I snore and dream of things
    that's in them catalogs,
To wake up kinder wishful
    for the coosie's mornin' call.
For breakfast at the wagon,
    and the round-up's daily brawl.

I'm batchin' at the Boar's Nest—
    my chair's a staple keg;
Jest the thought of canned termaters
    makes my paunch set up and beg!
The coyote howls
    and hears his kind respond acrost the draw,
And even my ol' ponies
    has each other's necks to chaw.

But if *I* squall—no answer
    but the bull bat's lonesome tune,
Or a skeered mouse on the table
    knockin' off a dirty spoon!
I ain't no hand for fancy chuck,
    I don't like crowds too well,
But batchin' in the Boar's Nest,
    it gits lonesomer than hell!

Classic Rhymes by S. Omar Barker

Canned Termaters

Them old time western cowboys
    mostly ate what they could git,
And drank what turned up handy,
    but I've heard them all admit
They sometimes got so tired of beans,
    of beef and even 'taters,
They'd purt near swap their saddles
    for a bait of canned termaters.
About the only stuff in cans
    them days was pork and beans,
Termaters, Eagle milk, and corn,
    and maybe some sardines;
And none of these was plentiful
    out where the cow trails ran,
For grub come mighty costly
    when you bought it in the can.
But sometimes in the wagon bed
    of big ranch operators
You'd maybe find a case or two
    of stuff called canned termaters.

Them old time cowhands
    never heard of vitamins an' such;
They never craved no fancy foods—
    at least not very much—
But, comin' in from cow-work
    where the dust was thick and hot,
Them juicy, cool termaters—well,
    they sure did hit the spot.
You even liked them better
    than you did dried apple pie,

And when your outfit furnished them,
   you sure was livin' high.
Why, even when you et in town,
   you shocked them restrunt waiters
By turnin' fancy vittles down
   and eatin' canned termaters!

A-batchin' in the boar's-nest,
   as the line camps then was called,
You often tired of cookin',
   and your appetite got stalled,
But if up there upon the shelf
   some canned termaters stood,
You'd "cut a can" for supper,
   and it sure did savor good.
Some days inside your slicker
   you would pack a can or two
Tied on behind your saddle.
   If the water holes was few
You'd "cut a can" and drink it
   as you jogged along the road,
And swear that canned termaters
   was the best fruit ever growed.

In town, the morning after
   you had helped the hoot owl hoot,
Your tongue would taste like leather
   from the top of some old boot,
Until you found a grocer
   that would trust you for a can,
And when you'd cut and drunk it,
   you was sure a diff'rent man.

That's how them oldsters tell it
    of the days when life was rough,
When ridin' men was rawhide men,
    and nothin' else but tough;
When men with hides and stummicks
    like on ol' bull alligator's,
Was still like kids for candy—
    when it come to canned termaters!

Power in the Pot

Of all the coffee drinkers that the world has ever knew,
There never was no one could beat the old time buckaroo.
His favorite rangeland rendezvous was 'round a steamin' pot
Containin' black jamoka plenty strong and plenty hot.
To suit his rawhide gullet called for purty potent stuff—
It had to float a horseshoe or it wasn't strong enough!

Bunkhouse Forum

The bunkhouse is a forum
    where the cowboys air their views
Upon most any subject
    that the mind of man could choose.
From fishworms to philosophy,
    they sure can get it told,
With the purest kind of logic
    for opinions that they hold.
You take, for instance, music,
    and what instruments the best:
Butch says he'll choose pianners
    and to hell with all the rest.
"They give so many tunes at once
    and ain't no trick to play.
Just poke your nickel in the slot
    and hear 'em bang away!"

Jiggs claims that fiddle music
    is the kind that can't be beat.
"It goes in at your ears," he says,
    "and comes out at your feet!"
"The git-arr," argues Curly,
    "sure will do to take along.
Just twang it kinder modest
    while you sing a cowboy song,
And if perchance your playin'
    isn't always up to snuff,
Nobody ever knows it—
    if your singin's loud enough!"

Bud argues that the harp of gold
    must be the best of all,
Because it's what the angels play.
    Ol' Slim lets out a squall.
"Now Bud," he says, "You're dealin'
    in the realm of vain deceit.
You'd *better* pick an instrument
    that's built to stand the heat!"
"The jew's harp," growls ol' Durkin,
    who would sour a pot of tea,
"That there's the only insterment
    I think I ever see
That's got some claim to virtue.
    It's the one I'd shorely choose,
Because it just ain't big enough
    to make it hard to lose!"

Ol' John, the coosie, sucks his pipe
    and pops rheumatic knees.
"You ain't asked my opinion, boys.
    I'll give it, if you please.
The world is full of insterments"—
    he blinks his one good eye—
"But mine's the good ol' mouth harp, boys,
    and now I'll tell you why.
Most insterments takes brains to learn—
    we'd all be out of luck—
But even cooks and cowboys
    ain't too dumb to blow and suck!
Now toot horns may be wonderful,
    no doubt the fiddle's gay,
But me, I'll choose the mouth harp,
    for it's all that I can play!"

Tenderfoot

You ask me: "What's a tenderfoot?"
    It ain't no word of shame.
In lots of ways a tenderfoot
    and cowboy are the same.
They've both got eyes, ears, nose and mouth,
    arms and legs and feet.
They both come wrapped in human skin,
    and both are made of meat.
They both will eat when hungry,
    they both will drink when dry,
And both will view a damsel
    with the same gleam in their eye.
They both, no doubt, are idols
    of some doting mother's heart,
But in the dust of cowcamps,
    they're a million miles apart.

You take a verdant tenderfoot
    and set him on a pony—
He occupies the saddle
    like a chunk of fresh baloney.
He wears a human noggin,
    so he must have human brains,
But to start his pony joggin',
    he will push upon the reins.
The only thing he seems to know
    about a horse is "Whoa!"
So the pony gits bewildered
    for it don't know where to go
Without the rider tells it
    by the use of rein or knee,
And to watch a greenhorn balk that horse
    is a dismal sight to see.

Classic Rhymes by S. Omar Barker

He may wear cowboy riggin's,
   but no matter what they cost,
The way he sets inside 'em
   looks like green corn after frost.
He can't read brands, he can't read sign,
   he gits lost in the hills;
He speaks of mares as horses,
   and he speaks of creeks as rills.
He's purt near always hungry
   when there ain't no chuck around.
He don't squat on his hunkers—
   he collapses on the ground.
He hollers "shoo!" at cattle,
   and in lots of other ways,
His lump of outdoor ignorance
   he charmingly displays.

He maybe plays good blackjack
   and can beat you bad at stud,
But like as not he thinks a horse,
   like cattle, chews his cud.
He'll maybe plumb outcuss you,
   and he may drink likker raw,
And whirl the gals
   as free as any man you ever saw.
Likewise his build is forked,
   and his chest may boast some hair,
But when it comes to cow work—well,
   the tenderfoot ain't there.
You ask me "What's a tenderfoot?"'
   He's human, I'll allow,
But mainly he's some feller
   who just *doesn't savvy cow!*

What the Ol' Texan Misses

Red cow, white-face, muley black,
   Yaller steer with a warbled back—
   Some grows lank an' some grows stocky,
   Some gits footsore where it's rocky.
   When I'm ridin' up an' down
   On the ranges fur frum town,
   I see many kinds of cattle:
   Some so pore their backbones rattle
   When they bawl, an' some so fat
   That their hips is broad an' flat.

   Purebred, scrubs, both horned an' muley,
   Some right gentle, some unruly.
   Plenty cattle runnin' out
   On the ranges, an' no doubt
   They're heap better beefers nowdays
   Than they was in old-time cow days;
   Yet old-timers, grizzled, lean,
   Boys that trailed frum Abilene,
   Tell me they find one sort missin'.
   Whut kind is it? Well, jest listen:

   Wild an' rangy, tall an' lank,
   Shag-haired fighter, thin of shank,
   Devil's cousin, shamble-trottin'—
   Mostly gone but not fergotten—
   Hide as tough as armor plate,
   Horns reached plumb acrost the state--
   On the plains o' wolf an' pronghorn
   How we miss the Texas longhorn!

   Red cows, white-face, muley blacks
   Trample dim fergotten tracks ....
   Longhorns ain't sech beef as Durham ....
   Jest the same, I'm lonesome fer 'em!

Old West Welcome

Upon the old-time ranches there was always table space
For any cowboy stranger droppin' in.
They never tried to judge him by the whiskers on his face,
Nor make him state his attitude toward sin.

They set him down to share their chuck,
    they gave his horse a feed
What brought him there they didn't ask to know.
They just showed hospitality in every word and deed.
They never asked him when he aimed to go.

To make the stranger welcome was a custom of the land
In which all cowfolks took an honest pride,
But this here obligation, you must also understand,
Implied a few things from the other side.

Suppose the stranger chose to stay one night or maybe two,
A week, a month—such time as he was there,
He pitched right in on any work his ranch host had to do,
And nearly always tried to do his share.

He might not be a cowhand of the rangeland's very best,
But if he showed he wasn't scared of sweat,
Nobody took exception to his stayin' as a guest,
Nor grudged him any vittles that he et.

Sometimes a stranger cowboy only aimed to stay the night
To rest himself and horse while driftin' through,
But found the boss could use a hand, he liked the work all right,
So wound up ridin' there a year or two.

The old-time western cowfolks never shut a stranger out
In summer's balm or blizzard's wintry storm.
Their ways was rough, their gizzards tough
    but don't you never doubt—
This world has known few hearts that was as warm!

Hospital Cowboy

They took me to a hospital
   to try and cure my itch.
"Twas there I learned the facts of life—
   at least some facts of which
A heap of cowboys ain't aware,
   a-ridin' on the range,
Until they've had some doctor
   try to cure them of the mange.

They throwed me on a narrow bunk
   a way up off the ground,
And after while a doctor
   and some nurses come around.
One stuck a needle in my arm
   and siphoned off some blood.
The doctor stuck me here and there,
   most any place he could,
Includin' the anatomy
   I set on when I ride,
With lady nurses lookin' on,
   and me no place to hide!

They slapped me on a table
   twice as hard as any plank
And photographed my innards
   from my goozlum to my flank.
They fed me, on some special chuck
   they said would keep me strong,
Then pulled a trick
   that didn't let me keep it very long.
They poured me full of buttermilk
   all thickened up with chalk.

Classic Rhymes by S. Omar Barker

They offered me a bath in bed,
  but there I had to balk.
I told 'em all I wanted
  was some salve to cure my itch,
So never mind to pamper me
  the way they would the rich.

One night a putty nurse come in
  to give my back a rub.
I told her such attention
  sorter made me out a scrub,
Because I always liked to pay
  such favors back in kind,
In case *her* back was achin'—
  but she said I needn't mind.
They took my pulse and temperature
  and both, I understand,
Was somewhat teeter-tottered
  when the nurses held my hand.

They done a heap to build me up,
  but first they tore me down.
They also learnt me how
  to wear a hind-before-most gown.
I went in there all mangy,
  but I come out sweet and pure,
As free of cowboy flavor
  as the stars are of manure.
The facts of life they learnt me
  would be purty hard to match,
But all they done to cure my itch
  was not to let me scratch!

Texas Zephyr

To figure how hard the wind blows
   Out on the Texas Plains,
   You hang a fresh-killed beef up
   With a pair of logging chains;
   And if, on the morning after,
   You find your beef's been skinned,
   And you have to ride to find the hide,
   There's been just a little wind!

Cowpuncher Caution

Old cowpunchers claim that you'd better not fool
   With a widow, a chuckwagon cook or a mule.
   The mule may seem gentle and full of good will,
   Then haul off and kick you plumb over the hill.
   The chuckwagon cook may not look very tough,
   But he'll slice off your ears if you tease him enough.
   The widow, she's kind to both you and your stock—
   And the first thing you know there's a cradle to rock!

"Purt Near!"

They called him "Purt Near Perkins,"
    for unless the booger lied,
He'd purt near done most everything
    that he had ever tried.
He'd purt near been a preacher
    and he'd purt near roped a bear;
He'd met up with Comanches once
    and purt near lost his hair.
He'd purt near wed an heiress
    who had money by the keg,
He'd purt near had the measles,
    and he'd purt near broke his leg.

He'd purt near been a trail boss,
    and accordin' to his claim,
He'd purt near shot Bill Hickok—
    which had purt near won him fame!
He'd purt near rode some broncs
    upon which no one else had stuck
In fact he was the feller
    Who had purt near drowned the duck!

Now mostly all the cowboys
    On the Lazy S B spread,
They took his talkin' with a grin
    And let him fight his head.
But one named Tom Maginnis
    Sorter told it to him rough:
"You're ridin' with an outfit now
    Where 'purt near' ain't enough!
We tie our lass ropes to the horn,
    An' what we ketch we hold,
And 'purt near' is one alibi
    We never do unfold!
In fact, right now
    I'll tell you that no word I ever hear
Sounds quite so plain damn useless
    As that little pair: 'purt near'!"

That's how ol' Tom Maginnis
    Laid it out upon the line,
And like a heap of preachin' talk,
    It sounded mighty fine.
But one day Tom Maginnis,
    While a-ridin' off alone,
He lamed his horse
    And had to ketch some neighbor nester's roan
To ride back to the ranch on.
    But somewhere along the way
A bunch of nesters held him up,
    And there was hell to pay!

Classic Rhymes by S. Omar Barker

Tom claimed he hadn't stole the horse—
    Just borrowed it to ride.
Them nesters hated cowboys,
    And they told him that he lied.
They cussed him for a horsethief
    And they'd caught him with the goods.
They set right out to hang him
    In a nearby patch of woods.
They had pore Tom surrounded,
    With their guns all fixed to shoot.
It looked like this pore cowboy
    Sure had heard his last owl hoot!

They tied a rope around his neck
    And throwed it o'er a limb,
And Tom Maginnis purt near knowed
    This was the last of him.
Then suddenly a shot rang out
    From somewhere up the hill!
Them nesters dropped the rope an' ran,
    Like nesters sometimes will
When bullets start to whizzin'.
    Tom's heart lept up with hope
To see ol' Purt Near Perkins
    Ridin' towards him at a lope.

"Looks like I purt near
    Got here just in time," ol' Perkins said,
"To see them nesters hang you!"
    Tom's face got kinder red.
"You purt near did!" he purt near grinned.
    "They purt near had me strung!
You're lookin' at a cowboy
    That has purt near just been hung!
And also one that's changed his mind—
    For no word ever said,
Can sound as sweet as 'purt near',
    When a man's been purt near dead!"

Rodeo!

Rodeo Days

Ropin' of yearlin's and tyin' em' down,
Wrastlin' of steers so the folks from town
Once in their lives gits a chance fer to see
Wild "hook 'em cowboys" like you and like me.

Straddlin' of broncos jest out of the chutes,
Forkin' 'em bareback like Injun Piutes,
Rakin' the shoulders of bellerin' steers,
Hearin' the audience whoopin' their cheers.

Milkin' wild cows and a-ridin' wild mules,
Wearin' silk shirts and a-yellin' like fools,
Cowboys is in from the ranches in dozens ,
Whoopin' 'em up fer their city cousins.

Dancin' all night and a-raisin' the deuce,
Millin' the streets like a loco cayuse—
Seems kinder funny fer us quiet boys
To raise so much rumpus and rouse so much noise!

Buckin' the contests we play at a battle
Learned on the ranges a-workin' with cattle.
What we put on ain't no circusy show,
It's workaday stuff, this here wild rodeo!

Makin' a game of rough skill and of muscles,
Lettin' America witness our tussels
Born of frontierin' and dear to the hearts
Of every old waddy in these western parts.

Rodeo time is fer rompin' and rarin'
Ridin' and ropin' and doin' yer darin'—
They say the cowboy is doomed fer to go—
Hi-yip! We've, still got the 'ol rodeo!

The Winner

I've got a black eye and a nose
    That's broke in three places or more!
They's patches of skin off my shin till it shows
    The bone, an' oh, golly, it's sore!

My lef' toe's swoll up in my boot,
    My hands only mittens could fit;
They's hints o' the prints of a horn yuh don't toot
    Somewhere jest about where I sit.

No, brother, it wasn't no wreck,
    Nor bronc ridin' that I've been in:
I jest done my best in a contest, by heck,
    A-milkin' wild cows—and I win!

Agreement in Principle

When a bronco gives way to his man-throwin' itch,
    In Texas they say that he lets in to "pitch";
While up in Wyoming, as no doubt you've heard,
    Them salty bronc peelers claim "buck" is the word.

Now this is a point you can argue, my friend,
    Till the last rope is raveled plumb out to the end,
But all hands agree that when broncos explode,
    It ain't what you call it that gits a man throwed!

Classic Rhymes by S. Omar Barker

Buckaroo's Squelch

Two buckaroos were rivals in the bronco ridin' game:
Ol' Breezy's brag was wild and loud, ol' Rusty's mild and tame.
"There ain't no use in talkin', boys," ol' Breezy used to boast,
"I've won top ridin' money everywhere from coast to coast
I've got ol' Rusty beat a mile at this here ridin' biz—
There ain't no use to argue, boys, for that's the way it is!"

Ol' Rusty never argued none, just rode 'em as they come,
A winnin' in some contests and a-losin' out in some,
But never braggin' any on his ridin', even when
He scored up in the money over mighty salty men.

Then one time at a rodeo, the way it come about,
The finals lay between them two. There wasn't any doubt
But what whichever one of them scored high that final day
Would win the big first money. Well, ol' Breezy drew a bay
Whose daddy was a wildcat and whose mammy was a snake.
Ol' Breezy come out skiddin' and he couldn't find the brake!
One jump he lost a stirrup and the next he lost his hat.
That bronco sure did learn him how to be an acrobat!

Ol' Breezy landed on his neck, he rode him on the rump,
But never hit the saddle more than every second jump.
The bronco didn't throw him off, but though the ride was funny,
It chalked him up "Disqualified"—and plumb outside the money.
Ol' Rusty drew a snaky dun as bad as Breezy's bay,
But set the saddle snug and tight and rode him anyway.

That evenin' at the payoff, watchin' Rusty draw his cash,
Ol' Breezy kept on braggin' might free and mighty brash.
"You rode it lucky *this* time," he declared, "but just the same,
I'm forkeder than you are at this bronco ridin' game!"

Ol' Rusty spoke up quiet like a heap of cowboys do,
And give his quiet answer to this braggin' buckaroo:
"Why, sure you are," he told him. "I agree with you, of course!
I only ride the saddle—you ride the whole danged horse!"

Four-Footed Dynamite

They asked me "What's a rodeo?"
    I told 'em that I knowed,
  But to put it into language was a job
    That had me throwed.
It's hoofs and horns and horse sweat,
    And the smell of western dust;
It's rannyhans to wrastle,
    And it's buckin' broncs to bust;
It's ropes to ketch a calf with.
    Piggin' strings to tie him down;
It's the daring-do of horseback men,
    The rangeland come to town.
It's Braymer bulls to straddle,
    And it's bones to bust and bruise;
It's Olympics of the saddle,
    If you win or if you lose.

It's men that pay an entrance fee
    For just a *chance* to win.
If all they win's a busted leg,
    They take it with a grin.
It's ropin' horses smart enough
    You'd think they'd been to school,
And so they have.
    It's years they've been in trainin', as a rule,
With some ol' cowboy teacher
    Usin' patience by the quart
To learn 'em how to ketch a calf
    And hold him like they ort.

Of course there's rules to go by,
   Just like any other game,
But the livestock sure can't read 'em,
   So it don't come out the same;
For though a ball game can be "throwed"—
   And sometimes is, I hear—
You can't buy off a buckin' bronc
   Nor "fix" a Braymer steer!

The wild West ain't as roomy
   As it was some years ago,
But still it sprouts adventure—
   So we've got the rodeo,
Where men that's knowed as cowboys
   Keep their horseback honor bright
By rope and spur and saddle,
   On four-footed dynamite!

What's a Bronco?

They asked me "What's a bronco!"
    Since they seemed to crave to know,
I kinder chawed it over,
    then I fed it to 'em slow.

"A bronc," I says, judicious,
    "which is what you mean, no doubt,
Is an equine son of cyclones
    with the hairy side turned out.
His soul is filled with cockleburs,
    and when this inward itch
Busts forth in outward action,
    he is said to 'buck' or 'pitch,'
Which means he comes unraveled,
    paws the moon to make it spin,
And agitates his muscles
    like he aimed to quit his skin.

One jump he views his belly,
    and the next he chins the stars.
Was you ever kicked by lightnin'?
    That's the way his landin' jars.
His color may be anything
    from black to flea-bit roan;
A sorrel, bay, or chestnut,
    he is still the devil's own
Until he's been unspizzled
    by some hairpin on his back
With two prongs hung acrost him
    and their juncture in the kack.

A pinwheel or a r'arback
    or a circlin' pioneer,
The bronc's a widow-maker
    when he throws himself in gear.
Though he's the toughest red meat
    you will ever come across,
If you're man enough to ride him,
    then you've got yourself a *hoss!*"

Mustang Manners

If you say that a cowboy got throwed off his bronc,
You sure ain't no range diplomat.
It's much more polite if you merely remark
That he got off to look for his hat!

The Riders

He claimed he'd rode the bad'uns
    plumb from Canada on south.
He'd rode 'em in the wet,
    and he'd rode 'em in the drouth.
He'd rode where broncs was little,
    and he'd rode where they was big,
And he wore a lot of purties
    made of silver on his rig.
Of course he'd never rode before
    for such a little spread,
But if they had some broncs to bust,
    he'd snap a few, he said.
The Boss, he kinder blinked his eyes
    and toed a piece of ground.
"Of course," he said, "us peelers here
    ain't never been around,
But if your pride can stand to ride
    amongst a bunch of hicks,
I'll hire you on, and maybe
    you can learn us all some tricks."

The stranger's name was Buck La Rue.
    He wore a fancy boot.
From all his talk you'd think
    he'd learned the hoot owl how to hoot.
But Joe, the ol' top peeler,
    always kinder held his jaw;
Just rode 'em as they came
    and never raised no big hurraw.
He cut La Rue some four-year-olds
    and watched him snap 'em out.
This Buck could fork a bronc,
    he said, there wasn't any doubt.

Classic Rhymes by S. Omar Barker

But when they talked of ridin'
   in the evenin's after chow,
'Twas Buck La Rue that never failed
   to tell the others how.
He'd say: "You made a middlin' ride
   upon that gray today,
But Joe, I've rode 'em awful tough,
   out Arizona way.
Of course you boys
   ain't been around enough to realize
That these here broncs is purty tame
   and kinder undersized.
I've forked 'em in Wyoming
   and the South Dakota hills,
That you've got to set 'em salty,
   or they jolt you to the gills."

But Joe just went on ridin',
   never puttin' on a show.
His spurs was never bloody,
   and you never heard him blow.
Then came a day when
   Buck La Rue got spilled upon the ground,
Because this roan bronc hadn't heard
   how Buck had been around.
"Why, damn his soul!" said Buck,
   and you could see it hurt his pride.
"This two-bit ranch can't raise a bronc
   that Buck La Rue can't ride!"

Buck screwed down on him once again.
    The roan unraveled quick,
And where he throwed ol' Buck that time,
    the dust was purty thick.

The third time that he throwed him,
    Buck's tongue forgot to wag.
Then ol' Joe spoke up quiet:
    "Let me try that little nag.
The chances are he'll throw me,
    for as Buck has often said,
I'm just a local rider
    for a little two-bit spread."

Joe stepped up in the saddle,
    raked the roan both fore and aft.
The bronc done plenty buckin',
    but ol' Joe set up and laughed:
"I'm just a pore ol' country boy,
    raised weak on country chuck.
Ain't never seen the elephant
    nor spun the world, like Buck!
Come on, ol' hoss, and show me
    how you lay 'em on the ground,
For, as ol' Buck has told you,
    I ain't never been around!"

That roan, he bucked the damnedest
    that a country bronco could,
But Joe stayed in the saddle,
    settin' deep down in the wood.
For once he done some spurrin'
    as he gave the boys a show,
While Buck just stood a-watchin',
    with his head hung kinder low.

Classic Rhymes by S. Omar Barker

Joe wrung him dry of buckin',
    like a wringer wrings a shirt,
Then stepped down from the saddle,
    lookin' plenty fresh and pert.

He says to Buck: "You take him,"
    and he give his hat a whirl.
"In case he's still too tough for you,
    just give him to your girl!"
The moral of this little tale,
    as some of you have guessed,
Is something most all cowpokes know,
    most everywhere out West;
For most of them have noticed
    that it's generally the case:
The toughest broncs are always those
    you've rode some other place.

Portrait of a Puncher

Dee Bibb's an ol' cowpoke I've known for some years.
He used to ride broncos and bulldog wild steers.
His name was well known in all rodeo camps
Where the dust of arenas was kicked up by champs.
When Dee took out after an ol' longhorn ox,
It was up to that bovine to ratttle his hocks,
Or Dee would sure ketch him, swing onto his head,
Clamp onto his antlers and put him to bed.
Then Dee would git up, and we'd know by his grin
That the ol' champ bulldogger had done it ag'in!

Dee also done ropin', and after each calf,
When he come to the chutes you could hear the boys laugh,
For Dee was one cowpoke who never did lack
For a good humored grin and a dry joke to crack.
With the skin off his nose or his back purt near broke,
He still had the makin's to build up a joke.
And whether luck tromped him or passed him the money,
Dee always found something in life that was funny.

Dee Bibb's an ol' cowpoke I've known quite a spell.
He trades cattle now and makes out purty well,
But whether he's solvent or whether he's busted,
His grin and good humor have never yet rusted.
He's big and he's brawny, though middle-aged now.
He savvies the horse and he savvies the cow.
He savvies the fiddle and also guitar.
He's got a nice fam'ly that's way above par.
He's just an ol' cowboy whose head is unbowed,
A neighborly feller who never acts proud,
A man you will notice in most any crowd,
'Cause he'll be the one that is grinnin' out loud!

One or the Other

The man who brags that he never got throwed
　Ain't one we much admire.
He's either, as cowpokes long have knowed,
　A tenderfoot or a liar!

A Cowpuncher Watches the Crowd

(Note: It was said that Tex Austin's Rodeo cowboys got more fun out of watching New Yorkers than the Gothamites did in seeing them perform.)

Hi, Pete! Yeah, I'm a-playin' corner post.
Lost! No, jest standin' herd and judgin' stock!
Why, sure! It's jest like sortin' cattle, Pete,
To watch folks come a-shovin' down the block.

Go to a show! Hell, no! What for! This here's
The show! It kinder makes me homesick, too.
Reminds me of Dogie William's' bunch—
All mixed—hey, look! Old Spotty's comin' through!
Doggone my hide, if that old girl ain't jest
The twin fer Dogie's pinto cow we found
Up Horse Thief Creek! Yeah—fat one there with furs.
See how she horns her way and holds her ground?
But looky, Pete! Jest like old Spot, she knows
Which ones won't take no hornin' from a cow.
She's edged her way around that muley bull—
I mean that necky banker—see 'em? Wow!

That there is a right pert heifer comin' by!
I'd say she's pure-bred Hereford from the way
She's slender at the ankles and still shows
She's built to carry meat. What did you say?
Quit starin'? Why, you scrub, these folks don't care
How much one pore cowpuncher reads their brands!
I ain't no more to them—not near as much—
As dudes is to Tom Talle's cows—or hands.

Classic Rhymes by S. Omar Barker

The Bronc Buster's Epitaph

Lies here where winds, sun rays an' rains
    Come beatin' o'er his head,
A bowleg son of western plains
    Whose name was Fork 'em Fred.

The bronco-stompers' grand cham-peen,
    He never pulled no leather.
He come out knockin' on 'em clean—
    Some hundreds altogether.

Life bucked him off—most likely down—
    Fer he was wild an' rowdy.
Too r'arin' fer to wear a crown
    Or tell St. Peter howdy.

Here lies pore Fred—no, that ain't right!
    I'll bet yuh, on the level,
He's raisin' hell in hell tonight
    Bronc-stompin' some pore Devil!

Horses and Cows

Classic Rhymes by S. Omar Barker

Horses Versus Hosses

I heard an old-time cowboy
    swappin' off some drawlin' talk
About them nags men used to ride,
    who didn't like to walk.
He spoke of them as *hosses*,
    so I up and asked him why
He didn't call them horses.
    Well, a gleam came in his eye,
And here is what he told me,
    be it right or be it wrong—
Some salty information
    that I'd like to pass along:

"You go out to the race track
    or some modern ridin' school,
And what you'll find 'em ridin'
    there is *horses*, as a rule.
You'll see nags wrapped in blankets
    when they raise a little sweat,
And bedded in warm stables
    so they won't git cold or wet.
Their saddle is a postage stamp;
    they're combed and curried slick.
Their riders bobble up and down
    like monkeys on a stick.
Them purty tricks are *horses*, son,
    but that there ain't the word
We used to call them shaggies
    that we rode behind the herd.
They might not be so purty,
    but they stayed outdoors at night.
They maybe weighed nine hundred pounds,
    all guts and dynamite.

They took you where you had to go
   and always brought you back,
Without no special rations
   that you purchase in a sack.
They loped all day on nothin'
   but your two hands full of grass.
On a straw hat full of water,
   they could climb a mountain pass.
They swum you through the rivers,
   and they plowed you through the sand—
You and your heavy saddle,
   and they learned to understand
Which end of cows the tail was on,
   till all you had to do
Was set up in the saddle
   while they did the cow work, too.
Sometimes they maybe dodged your rope,
   sometimes they bucked you high,
But they was sure the apple
   of the old-time cowboys eye!
These stable-pampered critters
   may be *horses*, sure enough,
But them old cow range *hosses*,
   they was born to take it tough.
So that's the way they took it,
   and they earned a tougher name
Than these here hand-fed horses,
   all so delicate and tame.
So you can have your horses
   with their hifalutin' gloss—
I'll take four-footed rawhide—
   or in other words, a *hoss!*"

Classic Rhymes by S. Omar Barker

Jughead

The Boss has bought some ponies,
    and you've drawed one in your string
That's a plumb tee-total stranger.
    Nary cowboy knows a thing
About his saddle histr'y—
    will he pitch or will he pace?
Will he drag it when you spur him?
    Will he blow up in your face?
You kinder look him over,
    and you note his Roman nose,
And the way he stands three-legged
    when he gits a chance to doze.
He's got them rollin' eyeballs—
    you can kinder see the whites,
An' he crowds in to the feed rack
    like his belly knowed its rights.
His under lip's a drooper—
    he's a jughead it appears.
He's a sorter shaggy sorrel,
    but he's got right purty ears.

He dodges when you rope him,
    and he ain't so easy led;
He humps up with the saddle,
    but he doesn't fight his head,
Nor try to dodge the bridle
    like he done the ketchin' noose.
You somehow git the idee
    that he figgers what's the use
Of wastin' all that energy
    to spook and snort around—
For like as not he's savin' it
    to strew you on the ground.

He swells up when you cinch him,
    so you've got to yank it tight.
He grunts some at the squeezin',
    but he don't try none to bite.
You've got him saddled easy,
    so you cheek him awhile you mount,
To see what kind of horse you've drawed
    and if he's any 'count.

You know he's broke to ride, of course,
    that don't signify
That he may not do some buckin'—
    and he does. It ain't so high,
But hell ain't got no hammer
    that could jolt a feller's seat
As hard as that ol' sorrel
    when he lands on all four feet!
Then, when he's done he's finished,
    and you ride him all day long,
Without no monkey-spookin'
    and he travels mighty strong.
There ain't no prancin' in him,
    and his gait ain't much for style,
But you kinder git to like him
    when you've rode him for awhile.
He bucks 'most every saddlin'
    just to prove he ain't no pet,
But it takes a full day's ridin'
    just to make that pony sweat.
There ain't much purty to him,
    but all hell ain't half as wide
As the ground his legs can cover
    in a single-saddle ride.

Classic Rhymes by S. Omar Barker

The Boss, he brought some ponies
    and he cut one to your string
That couldn't beat a burro
    in a fancy horse-show ring;
Yet when the trail is tough and long,
    you set up in your kack
And thank the Lord for Jughead
    for he'll git you there—and back!

The Unpardonable Sin

There's things that make a cowboy mad,
    And some of them are trivial.
He may be quite a touchy lad
    When things get too convivial.

But if you want to see him when
    He's really got his fur up,
Return a borrowed saddle with
    The length changed in his stirrup!

Buckaroo Braggin'

Cowboys may do some braggin'
　When they're gathered 'round the wagon,
　　For the western buckaroo is human, too;
But of the things he's proud of—
The ones he brags out loud of—
　　You'll mostly find they number mighty few.

He may boast just a little
Of his skill with pot and kittle,
　　For most all cowpokes savvy how to cook.
He might brag on his ramblin'
Or claim that in his gamblin'
　　He's the kind of guy no tinhorn ever took.

In case he's feelin' cheerful,
He may talk a modest earful
　　About the many gals he's left behind;
And maybe, with some giggin,
He will boast about his riggin'
　　And the classy saddles that his pants have shined.

His pride in his rough callin'
Don't require much caterwaulin'—
　　He's the most unbraggin' cuss you'll come across;
But you mighty sure can figger
That no brag is ever bigger;
　　Than a cowboy's when he's braggin' on his hoss!

Classic Rhymes by S. Omar Barker

Some Horses I Have Rode

I've rode a heap of horses, and a few of them were fools.
A few were rockygaited and another few were mules.
A few were fancy horseflesh that it cost a heap to own,
In colors all the way from black to Appaloosa roan.
A few were hammer-headed, and a few were hard to set,
But purt near all had special traits that I remember yet.
Ol' Prince was just a workhorse that I straddled as a kid,
Without no saddle half the time, but everything he did
Was with a willing spirit, whether tugging at a plow
Or busting over mountain trails to chouse a dodging cow.
Now Fanny was a little bay that throwed me once or twice.
Her step was light and airy, and she held her head up nice.

To ketch out in the pasture, ol' Spike was quite a scamp,
But he sure did savvy cow work, and he always stayed in camp.
Gray Frankie was a sweetie, sure-footed as a bear,
And Dixie was my brother's faithful lion-hunting mare.
Ol' Bill was built right beefy, yet he took a heap of pride
In stepping gay and frolicsome when saddled up to ride.
Smart Nick, our palomino, till he got cut on the wire,
Was gaited like a rockin' chair beside a cozy fire,
Yet still as tough a cowhorse as you'd ever want to straddle,
And prouder than a peacock of his looks beneath a saddle.

I've rode myself some horses, and I hope to ride some more
Before the Big Boss tallies off my final ridin' score.
Ol' Johnny, Dempsey, Trigger—I don't aim to name them all—
The build of some of them was short, the build of others tall.
In some the blood was mustang, and in some the breeding good,
But most of them most always seemed to do the best they could;
And that, my friends, is something that may not be quite so true
Of all the well-known human race—including me and you!

Watchin' Him Drink

When you ride a horse to water,
    Slack the reins and let him drink,
You can learn a heap about him
    That you maybe might not think.
If he kinder blows the water,
    And he drinks in little sips.
He's a dainty, lightsome stepper,
    And he seldom ever slips.
It's ten to one he's kind at heart
    And nickers for his feed;
Don't need no spurs to make him go
    And never hard to lead.

You take a horse that gulps it
    Like his belly couldn't wait,
He's likely stumble-footed,
    But he'll pack a heap of freight.
The one that socks his muzzle
    In 'most halfway to his eyes,
He's hard-jawed to the bridle,
    And he'll never take a prize
For speed nor spizz nor spirit,
    But when all the rest are tirin',
You'll find his guts is rawhide,
    And his legs is made of iron.

The way some ponies skitter
    When you ride 'em to a pool,
You'd think they never drank before,
    The way they act the fool.
But such a horse is handy
    When there's tricky swales to ride.
He just won't never bog you,
    And he won't git alkalied.
You ride a horse to water,
    And the different ways they drink.
May help you git a line
    Upon the ways they act and think.

You set up in the saddle,
    And you sorter figger out
How one's a good one 'cause he's quick,
    Another 'cause he's stout.
The willin' ones,
    The lazy, the smart ones, and the dumb—
You ponder on their drinkin',
    And no doubt it helps you some
To understand their habits
    In the way a cowboy should.
But ain't it kinder funny
    That you mostly find 'em good?
Well, no, it ain't so funny,
    and you know it, too, becuz
If he wasn't good for *som'ethin'*,
    You'd be ridin' one that wuz!

Namin' The Broncos

You take a ranch *remuda*, and the names them ponies wear
Have got so much variety it makes you wonder where
They ever got their titles—like Chino, Chug, or Scat,
Or Chicken Wire or Capulin, and other names like that.
You find one hoss named Buckshot and another Whiskey Pete,
Or maybe one called Wagon Wheel, and one called Wagon Sheet.
Wild Bill—of course his namesake was a well-known shootin' man,
And Clabber for a white hoss you can easy understad.

Ol' Bullfrog, he's a jumper and Ol' Two-Step likes to prance,
And Polkadot, he's spotted—you can see that at a glance.
But Silver Dollar, I B Dam, Dishwater, Tattlebum
Are names that make you meditate upon just how they come.
Well, cowboys don't set up all night to think up names for nags.
They'll call a fast hoss Lightnin', and Molasses one that lags.
Sand Sifter is a pacer, an ol' Spooky one that shies.
Or Bally, Paint, and Chalkeye, they ain't hard to analyze.

But cow ranch names of hosses, the best ones and the worst,
A pony mostly gits 'em from the man who rides him first.
Of course that man's the peeler. When he busts a bronco colt,
Offhand he calls him something, and the name just takes a-holt
Take Capulin—that's Spanish for a wild chokecherry bush.
A bronco tangles in one, and he's named right from the push.
A-sidlin' past the cookshack on a "second saddle" ride,
A bronc gits spooked by water that the coosie throws outside.
So when the peelers schooled him out and got him saddle-tame,
It comes out sure as shootin' that Dishwater is his name!
Sometimes them peelers may git throwed
    and land no tellin' where—
I knowed a sorrel cowhoss once whose name was Prickly Pear!

You take a ranch remuda, and the name of every hoss
Is knowed alike to wrangler, to the hands and to the boss.
It may be somethin' simple or it may be Tattlebum—
You better ask the peeler if you want to know how come.

The Sparkin' Plug

Give me a nervous highstrung hoss,
    keen eyed, sharp eared an' swift
To ride when cuttin' cattle from a herd;
    A rangy ol' long legged dun to follow when they drift,
That don't git too excited when he's spurred.

A fast but calm an' gentle mount to straddle when I rope,
    An' strong enough to drag 'em to the fire.
Fer night herd give me some o' plug that's got a lazy lope
    An' don't git scared in case yuh hit a wire.

Fer roundin' up an' drivin' strays up where the country's rough,
    I like to ride a sturdy chested bay.
Fer runnin' after rustlers where the goin's fast an' tough,
    Give me a glass-eyed pinto any day!

But when some evenin' brings a chance fer me to ride to her,
    Give me a runnin' hoss with wind to spare
Or else whatever's handy with four legs an' ribs to spur—
    Fer sparkin—*any kind that gits me there!*

The White Mustang

(The legend of the ghost horse of the plains was first written about by Washington Irving.)

    Wherever rhythmic hoofbeats drum,
      As galloping riders go or come,
      Wherever the saddle is still a throne,
      And the dust of hoofs by wind is blown,
      Wherever are horsemen young or old,
      The Pacing Mustang's tale is told.

      A hundred years on hill and plain,
      With comet-tail and flying mane,
      Milk-white, free, and high of head,
      Over the range his trail has led.
      Never a break in his pacing speed,
      Never a trot nor a lope his need,
      Since faraway days of the wagon train,
      Men have followed his trail in vain.

Classic Rhymes by S. Omar Barker

A score of horses spurred to the death,
Still he flees like a phantom's breath,
And from some hill at horizon's hem,
Snorts his challenge back at them.
A bullet drops him dead by day,
Yet white at night he speeds away.
Forever a thief of tamer steeds,
Stallion prince of the mustang breeds,
Coveted prize of the men who ride,
Never a rope has touched his hide.

Wherever the saddle is still a throne,
The Great White Mustangs tale is known.

O Phantom Ghost of heart's desire,
Lusty-limbed with soul of fire,
Milk-white Monarch, may you, free,
Race the stars eternally!

Longhorn

They asked me "What's a longhorn?" . . .
    Well, I didn't tell it scarey—
Just told 'em "Whyn't you look it up
    in some good dictionary?"
But when they come and told me
    that the best that they could find
Was "a Texas cow with lengthy horns,"
    I up and spoke my mind.

Of course his horns was lengthy—
    you could guess that from his name,
But that ain't all his ticket
    to the hall of western fame.

Classic Rhymes by S. Omar Barker

The longhorn steer was covered
   by a hide so tough and thick
That just to get a toe-holt,
   it would take a Texas tick
A steady week of borin'
   every day and every night,
And dull his apparatus
   till he couldn't chaw a bite!

It's true he wasn't purty—
   this Texas longhorn steer—
But them there bony shanks of his
   could plumb outrun a deer.
His backbone was a ridge pole
   that was sometimes sorter swayed.
He fought both wolves and panthers
   with a courage undismayed.
His neck was long and leathery,
   his ribs as flat as planks.
He mostly wore his belly
   kinder tucked up in his flanks.
His shoulder ridge was sharp enough
   to split a hailstone through,
And when it come to hidin' out,
   he knowed just what to do
To make the cowboy trouble,
   both to find and bring him in
Which maybe is one reason
   why them brush hands growed so thin.

His color pattern varied,
 sometimes kinder dull and dead,
But the blood that coursed his rawhide veins
 was reddest of the red.
His hoofs, just like the devil's,
 they was split enough to clack.
Acrost the page of history
 they trailed a deathless track.
His nose could smell a norther
 like a bee can smell perfume,
And when his kind stampeded,
 you had better give 'em room!
He wasn't just a bovine,
 but a wild breed all his own,
With a stubborn love of freedom
 bred in every breath and bone.
He trod out countless cattle trails
 to mark a frontiers dawn,
Till plows and rails and fences
 come along to shove him on.

You ask me "What's a longhorn?"
 Well, just one more word's enough:—
The longhorn *made* the cowboy—
 and he made him plenty tough!

The Female of the Species

It's a well-knowed fact in the range country
 That a he calf bellers heap worse than a she.
Or, in other words, fer to be plumb clear,
 A heifer stands brandin' heap calmer than a steer.
But say, when they're up and a puncher tries to ride 'em
Fer to have him a little mite o' fun,
The heifers they buck like they's dynamite inside 'em,
Or a Hades come undone!

Well, the steer bucks, too, but he don't cut loose
A-raisin' the gosh-almighty deuce,
Like the she-stuff does, when, a-lookin' right mild,
They takes a sudden notion fer to act up wild.
A old Ma cow, she kin fight a heap fiercer
Than the wust old bull on the range!
Her hookin's are more plentiful
   an' her bluffin' much skeercer
Than her husband's—ain't that strange!

It's likewise said that a bronco mare
Kin throw a bronc buster farther up in the air,
Kin buck a heap wuss an' raise more hell,
An' travel hard trails fer a longer spell.
It reminds me o' readin' somewheres by a poet—
Was it Kipperling—lemme see?—
That the she-stuff (shorely ever'body ought to know it!)
Is a waspier breed than the he!

Cowpen Moo-Sic

They asked me: "What's a beller?"
    Well, a beller is a bawl
That ain't exactly like a *moo*
    nor yet quite like a squall.
An ol' cow moos to coax her calf
    from close by in the brush.
She *bawls* all night at weanin' time,
    until you wish she'd hush.
But when she bellers that's a sound
    that's got a heap more meanin'
Than just plain cowpen moo-sic
    that you hear when calves are weanin'.

For instance, let a range cow
    smell fresh blood from some dead critter—
It's then she sure 'nough bellers
    like she thinks all hell would git her.
Her tongue shoots out about a foot,
    and them weird sounds she makes
Sound terrible enough to give a man
    the chills and shakes.
Then all the cattle roundabout
    come snuffin' at a trot
To help her beller for the dead,
    and when they reach the spot,
There ain't no squall the banshee makes
    will make your neck hair rise
Like that there bovine blood call
    as it echoes to the skies.
And if among the mourners
    some ol' bull joins in the tune,
'Twill purt near melt the marrow
    of the man up in the moon.

Of course, you know it's really
    just a harmless bovine sound
But deep inside it shakes you
    like an earthquake shakes the ground.
Well, that's one kind of beller,
    and another that I'll name
Is two range bulls a-talkin' fight.
    Although it ain't the same,
It's also gizzard-stirrin' to a man
    with cowboy ears,
Who understands the language
    of the rangeland sounds he hears.
For though most plain steer bawlin'
    may be just a restless notion,
The sure 'nough beller is a sound
    of plumb raw cow emotion.

A calf may beller
    when he's roped or branded, and a cow
Will beller when she's on the prod.
    I better tell you how
To tell a beller from a bawl.
    It ain't alone the sound.
A bawl is mostly pointed up,
    a beller towards the ground;
And also, if on "beller facts"
    you're still somewhat in doubt,
A bawl becomes a beller
    when its tongue is stickin' out!

The Last Trail

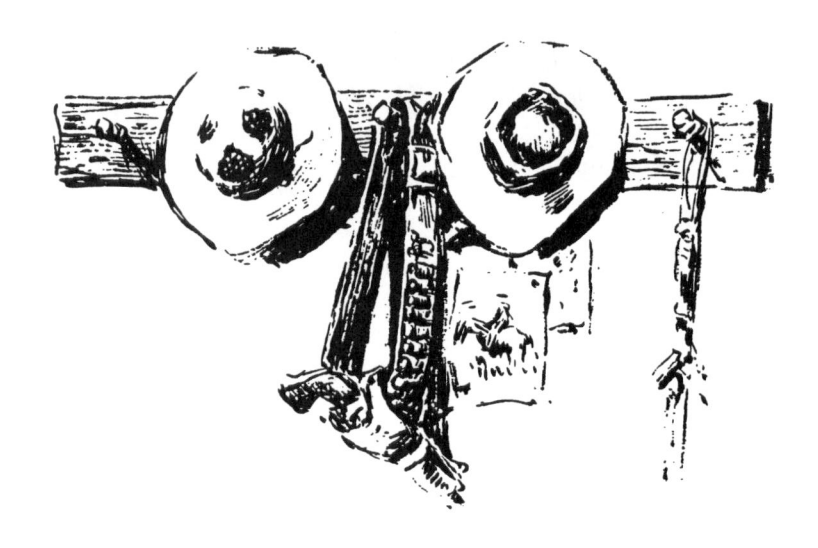

Classic Rhymes by S. Omar Barker

The Last Bronc

Buckskin, black, mohina, gray,
R'arin' roan or buckin' bay—
Ever' bronc cut to yore string,
Mount him, cowboy, with a swing!
Some you'll straddle wide and high,
Some will buck you to the sky.
Snortin' outlaws, broncs or just
Unbroke colts to tame and bust,
In yore string by luck or Fate,
Ride 'em, boy, don't hesitate!
Life's a ridin' contest, boy,
Some draws grief and some draws joy.
One old bronc we all must straddle,
Great big black without no saddle.
He's the contest's final draw,
Shadow-eyed and dark with awe.
Big Jedge watchin'—swing up, son!
Show Him you ain't scared of none!
White horse, sorrel, pinto, too—
Ride 'em all, and when you're through,
Throw yore leg acrost the back
Of old Univarsal Black.

Ride Him like you've always rode—
Never fear, you won't git throwed!

Set him clean and scratch him fast:
Bronco Death, the contest's last!

Adios!

In a valley high up in the mountains,
 With the wind like a knife on their cheeks,
They carried ol' Mac to his resting,
 When winter lay white on the peaks.

Behind come his favorite ol' pony,
 Led slow by an ol' Spanish friend.
The saddle and chaps, they was empty—
 Ol' Mac's trail had come to its end.

There wasn't no fancy procession—
 Just cowboys and Injuns and such—
Plain men of the saddle and mountains,
 And nobody said very much.

Ol' Dough-Belly Price done the preachin',
 Astride of his cream-yaller hoss.
All he said was a few words and simple
 About Mac, the ol' wagonboss.

"We've not come slicked up for a show-off,
 We've not brought no preacher to pray.
My words won't be fancy ones, neither,
 For Mac wouldn't want it that way.

"We all of us knew Mac McMullen.
 I couldn't say more if I'd try.
He was one of our own, but he's left us.
 We've gathered to tell him goodbye.

Classic Rhymes by S. Omar Barker

"The range that he rode was a wide one,
   His friendships was many and deep;
So now that his saddle is empty,
   God rest him at ease in his sleep!"

'Twas thus near old Taos in the mountains,
   With winter-white peaks looming close,
They carried a *man* to his resting,
   And quietly said *"Adios!"*

Old Cowboy

Here's an old cowboy setting' in the sun,
  Silent as the plains when day is done;
  Settin' here a-smokin' by a ranch house door
  Bones too bent an' brittle fer the roundup any more.

  All the words he wants to say have long been said
  Now he's thumbin' picture books in his head:
  Picture books the long years make for him,
  Clear and bright to look at through eyes dim.

  Picture books where young men brown an' strong,
  Fight stampedes with a shoutin' song.
  Scenes where the old Rio Grande runs
  'Neath splashin' hoofs and smokin' guns.

  Scenes so far off past that he
  Dreams of them as still to be.

  Cowboy eyes from other days
  Inward looking at old ways—
  Western ways of horse an' gun—
  See their ridin' jest begun.

  Old men's dim old eyes see strange
  Phantom riders on the range.
  Dreaming old 'uns by the door
  Ride forth brave with youth once more.

Classic Rhymes by S. Omar Barker

To an Old Cowboy—Departed
(Jim Whitmore)

One more old saddle empty now,
    One more old cowboy gone,
No more to talk of horse and cow,
    No more to see the dawn
Rise red across wide mesas where
    The slim gray coyotes cry,
No more to smell brand-burning hair
    Beneath cow-country sky.

No more to ride a homeward lane,
    Nor calculate the grass,
Nor estimate a cloud for rain—
    So the oldtimers pass.
Adios, amigo. We shall hear
    In memory a cowboy yell
Re-echoing its rawhide cheer
    In hearts that knew it well.

Gone to the wagon from this land
    Of hardy horseback men.
Your grin was kindness, your warm hand
    We shall not clasp again.

Adios, Jim! New names . . . . new faces,
    But yours remembered still
In all the old familiar places
    Of cowcamp, trail and hill!

An Old Cowhand Enters Heaven

Ol' Texas Charley lay on his bed,
    His hair plumb white with years,
A-tallyin' memories through his head
    Like a herd of longhorn steers.

Recallin' scents and sights and sounds
    That a cowhand can't forget:
Cattle asleep on the beddin' ground . . . .
    The smell of a horse's sweat . . .
The campfire talk of a roundup crew,
    With the long day's ridin' done. . . .
Curly mesquite grass pearled with dew
    At the dawn of a Texas sun.

Under the covers it seemed to him
    His legs could feel once more
Saddle and horse, on a mesa's rim
    Where eagles lift and soar.

His time was short and friends stood by
    They spoke of an angel band
A-waitin' with welcome beyond the sky,
    To take him by the hand.

But Texas Charley's eyes was bright
    With a sight they couldn't see.
He said: "Folks, I'll make out all right
    Don't fret none over me.
For instead of angels, milky-skinned,
    A-playin' their golden harps,
I see grass wavin' in the wind,
    An' cowboys sunnin' tarps . . ."

His face lit up plumb beautiful,
　　And we knowed he had come to taw,
A-hearin' some ol' longhorn bull
　　A-bellerin' down the draw!

The Last Lone Trail

It ain't as if lone trails was new to me—
    The desert's ways has been my ways
Since jest a boy a-hankerin' to live free,
    I drifted dreamin' in the haze
On lonesome mesas where the sun
    Sets friendly-like when day is done.

Stars was my pardners and old night a friend—
    It ain't as if from some tight room
Into' the Great Gray Range without no end
    I'd step a-shiverin' in the gloom—
Now I'm to go it seems right good—
    I wouldn't turn back if I could.

It ain't as if adventurin' was new
    To me: my life's pack has been light
Along far trackless trails. So is it, too,
    Now that I drift again tonight.
The rangeland where man-trails are dim
    Somehow jest touches, rim to rim,

God's Great Gray Desert, and I find
    His Last Lone Trail friendly and .... kind.

Alphabetical Index of Poems

A Cowboy's Christmas Prayer 122
A Cowpuncher Watches the Crowd 172
A Frontier Wife. 103
A Gal to Spark 66
A Letter From Judge Bean 53
A Measure for Man. 27
Adios! 196
Against the Dark 43
Agreement in Principle 160
An Old Cowhand Enters Heaven 200
Bear Ropin' Buckaroo. 138
Bedtime Story 87
Big Windies. 20
Black Magic 132
Boar's Nest Batcher 141
Boy into Man. 94
Bruin Wooin'. 63
Buckaroo Braggin'. 180
Buckaroo's Coffee 133

Buckaroo's Squelch 161
Bunkhouse Forum. 146
Bunkhouse Thanksgiving 111
Canned Termaters 143
Code of the Cow Country 26
Cow Country 129
Cowboy Breed 28
Cowboy Ridin' 17
Cowboy's Complaint 24
Cowboy's New Year's Resolutions 126
Cowboy's Reverie. 57
Cowpen Moo-Sic 192
Cowpuncher Caution 154
Cowpuncher Praise 107
Cry, Coyote! 39
Curly Wolf College 101
Draggin' in the Tree 118
Drifter's Thanksgivin'. 113
Drylander's Christmas. 125
Fine! 45
Fireside Windies 140
Four-Footed Dynamite 162
Grand Canyon Cowboy 30
Granger's Daughter. 58
Grass 32
Grave Error. 49
Gun Law 48
Hangin'. 47
His First Shave 106
His Night-Herd Pardner 40
Horse Corral Etiquette. 33
Horses Versus Hosses. 175
Hospital Cowboy 152
Hot Ir'n!. 134
Hunted Men 34
Into the West. 38
Jack Potter's Courtin'. 70
Judge Bean's Bear. 50
Judge Bean's Jury. 46

Jughead	177
Jurisdiction	52
Line-Camp Christmas Letter	120
Longhorn	188
Manana	30
Mariposa Mesa	62
Mountain Ranch Wife	102
Mustang Manners	165
Namin' The Broncos	184
Ol' Snoozy Schmidt	25
Old Cowboy	198
Old Wagon Tracks	42
Old West Welcome	151
One or the Other	171
One Way of Proposin'	76
Outlaw's Funeral	36
Pants Polisher	18
Portrait of a Puncher	170
Power in the Pot	145
"Purt Near!"	155
Quittin' Talk	136
Ranch House Night	104
Ranch Mother	96
Ranchman's Widow	100
Rangeland Perfume	73
Rangeland Sleepin'	41
Ravens Over the Pass	108
Rodeo Days	159
Some Horses I Have Rode	181
Sometimes Serious	23
Spurs	37
Stew-Pified	77
Tall Men Riding	15
Tenderfoot	148
Texas Truth	33
Texas Zephyr	154
Thanksgiving Argument	116
The Bronc Buster's Epitaph	173
The Chuckwagon	130

The Cowboy's Religion 124
The Cowgirl at College 105
The Deputy's Star 74
The Empty Bunk 79
The Female of the Species 191
The Last Bronc 195
The Last Lone Trail 202
The Riders 166
The Ring-Tailed Wowser 89
The Sentimental Banker 68
The Sparkin' Plug 185
The Tie-Fast Men 16
The Unpardonable Sin 179
The White Mustang 186
The Winner 160
Thirsty Cowboy 60
Three Wise Men 91
To a Blue-Eyed Cowgirl 78
To a Mountain Cowgirl 61
To an Old Cowboy—Departed (Jim Whitmore) 199
Trail Dust 31
Useless Question 33
Vaquero's Valentine 85
Watchin' Em Ride 97
Watchin' Him Drink 182
Wearin' Daddy's Hat 88
Weddin' in Texas 81
What the Ol' Texan Misses 150
What's a Bronco? 164

Order Form

❏ Yes! Please send me the following merchandise.

Name_____
Address_____
City_____ State_____ Zip_____
Phone_____ Fax_____

Title	Qty.	Each	Total
Cowboy Poetry, Classic Rhymes by S. Omar Barker Edited by Mason & Janice Coggin and Jon Richins	_____	$19.95	_____
The Pioneer Squire Barker Family, Life and times of the Barker family 1889–1995 by Jodie & Bob Phillips	_____	$ 9.95	_____
Songs and Poems of S. Omar Barker (audio cassette) sung and recited by Jon Richins	_____	$10.00	_____
Rawhide Rhymes, Poems by S. Omar Barker (audio cassette) recited by Andy Hedges	_____	$10.00	_____
Cowboy Poetry, Classic Rhymes by Bruce Kiskaddon, comp. by Mason and Janice Coggin	_____	$14.95	_____
Coggin does Kiskaddon, Cowboy Poetry Classics Vol. 1 (audio cass.) recited by H. Mason Coggin	_____	$10.00	_____
SAVE! Combination Kisdaddon book and Kiskaddon audio cassette	_____	$22.00	_____
SAVE! Combination Barker poetry book and either Barker audio cassette (Please underline either Hedges or Richins here)	_____	$28.00	_____
	Subtotal		_____
Arizona residents include 7% sales tax.	Tax		_____
Please add $3.00 for the first item, plus $1.50 for each additional item for shipping and handling.	S&H		_____
Foreign orders must be accompanied by a postal money order in U.S. funds.	TOTAL		_____

Send check or money order to: Cowboy Miner Productions
P.O. Box 9674, Phoenix, Arizona 85068
To order by phone call (602) 944-3763. Ask about quantity discounts.